PRAISE FOR *MALIK AMBAR*

"In a lively and well-researched narrative, Omar H. Ali follows the footsteps of an exceptional man while painting a vivid portrait of a unique and complex society molded by the cultures, languages, and religions of multiple continents. It is a fascinating story of slavery, freedom, power, and transformations."

—Sylviane A. Diouf, *Director of the Lapidus Center for the Historical Analysis of Transatlantic Slavery and Curator at the Schomburg Center for Research in Black Culture of The New York Public Library*

"While the story of Malik Ambar's fascinating life is a key to understanding major cultural and political exchanges across the Indian Ocean, it is also the moving and inspiring tale of an African boy who grows up to become an Indian king. This succinct biography by Omar Ali allows the reader to plunge into the cosmopolitan world of the Deccan courts, where Abyssinian slaves and noblemen played an important role in political and military affairs. Ambar's talents, which extended from warfare to diplomacy, placed him at the center of events that shaped the seventeenth century. This book adds new perspectives to his early life and the complex forces that took him across the Indian Ocean, and offers fresh insight into how he found his place in India."

—Navina Haidar, *Curator, Department of Islamic Art, The Metropolitan Museum of Art*

MALIK AMBAR

SERIES EDITOR: Bonnie G. Smith, Rutgers University

Published
ANWAR al-SADAT: *Transforming the Middle East*
Robert L. Tignor

MUSTAFA KEMAL ATATÜRK: *Heir to an Empire*
Ryan Gingeras

MARGARET THATCHER: *Shaping the New Conservatism*
Meredith Veldman

QUEEN VICTORIA: *Gender and Empire*
Susan Kingsley Kent

MALIK AMBAR: *Power and Slavery Across the Indian Ocean*
Omar H. Ali

SIMONE DE BEAUVOIR: *Creating a Feminist Existence in the World*
Sandrine Sanos

Forthcoming
LIN ZEXU: *Imperial China in a Globalizing World*
David Atwill

THE LIVES OF PEOPLE and the unfolding of earth-shaking events inspire us to love history. We live in a global age where big concepts such as "globalization" often tempt us to forget the "people" side of the past. The titles in *The World in a Life* series aim to revive these meaningful lives. Each one shows us what it felt like to live on a world historical stage and even to shape the world's destiny.

The lives of most individuals are full of activity and color and even passion and violence. The people examined in *The World in a Life* series often faced outsized challenges, but they usually met the great events of their day energetically. They lived amidst enormous change, as we often do. Their lives show us how to navigate change and to find solutions. They made fateful decisions, often with much soul-searching or—as often—on the spur of the moment and even intuitively. We have much to learn from these fateful past lives.

Their actions, however, were filled with complexity. Biographies in this series give a "nutshell" explanation of how important paradoxes and dilemmas have been in the stories of individuals operating on the world stage. Their lives become windows onto the complicated trends, events, and crises of their time, providing an entry point for a deeper understanding of a particular historical era. As such events and crises unfolded, these historical figures also faced crises in their personal lives. In the intertwined dramas of the personal and political, of the individual and the global, we come to understand the complexities of acting on the world stage and living in world history.

BONNIE G. SMITH

THE WORLD IN A LIFE

MALIK AMBAR

POWER AND SLAVERY ACROSS THE INDIAN OCEAN

OMAR H. ALI

New York   Oxford
OXFORD UNIVERSITY PRESS

Oxford University Press is a department of the University of Oxford.
It furthers the University's objective of excellence in research,
scholarship, and education by publishing worldwide.

Oxford   New York
Auckland   Cape Town   Dar es Salaam   Hong Kong   Karachi
Kuala Lumpur   Madrid   Melbourne   Mexico City   Nairobi
New Delhi   Shanghai   Taipei   Toronto

With offices in
Argentina   Austria   Brazil   Chile   Czech Republic   France   Greece
Guatemala   Hungary   Italy   Japan   Poland   Portugal   Singapore
South Korea   Switzerland   Thailand   Turkey   Ukraine   Vietnam

For titles covered by Section 112 of the US Higher Education
Opportunity Act, please visit www.oup.com/us/he for the
latest information about pricing and alternate formats.

Published by Oxford University Press
198 Madison Avenue, New York, New York 10016
http://www.oup.com

Library of Congress Cataloging-in-Publication Data
Ali, Omar H. (Omar Hamid), author.
    Malik Ambar : power and slavery across the Indian Ocean / Omar H. Ali.
        pages cm. -- (The World in a Life)
    Includes bibliographical references and index.
    ISBN 978-0-19-026978-4 (pbk., acid free : alk. paper)   1. Malik 'Ambar,
1549–1626. 2. Africans--India--Biography. 3. Marshals--India--Deccan--
Biography. 4. Ahmadnagar (Kingdom)--Officials and employees--Biography.
5. Deccan (India)--History. I. Title. II. Series: The World in a Life.
    DS461.9.M25A45 2016
    954.8025092--dc23

                                                        2015020911

FOR MY ABU, WITH LOVE

CONTENTS

LIST OF ILLUSTRATIONS

LIST OF MAPS

KEY FIGURES

MUGHAL

Jalal ud-din Muhammed Akbar (1542–1605)—Mughal emperor. He is Ambar's main rival among the Mughals.

Jahangir (1569–1627)—Mughal emperor; Prince Nur-u-din Muhammed Salim.

Nur Jahan (1577–1645)—Wife of Emperor Jahangir who took over much of the workings of government.

Shah Jahan (1592–1666)—Mughal emperor, who rebelled against his father Jahangir while he was prince.

Mirza Asad Beg—Mughal envoy who meets with Malik Ambar.

Prince Daniyal—Sent by Akbar in 1595 to Bijapur to remind Burhan of his proper place on the empire's frontier.

Prince Murad—Son of Akbar, by whom he was sent in 1595 to Ahmednagar to capture the fort through siege warfare.

Prince Khusrau—Son of Jahangir, who led a rebellion but was caught and then blinded by his father.

Khan-Khanan (Abdur Rahim)—General of Mughal armies who is at war with Ambar and the Deccani forces. He was one of Akbar's nine Ministers (*Diwan*) in his court.

Shah Nawaz Khan (Iraj)—The son of Abdur Rahim. He was a Mughal commander in Jahangir's army and defeated Malik Ambar in 1616.

Abu'l-Fazl ibn Mubarak—Principal author of the *Akbarnama*, The Book of Akbar.

Mu'tamad Khan—Court chronicler of *Tuzuk-i Jahangiri*, Memoirs
of Jahangir, who acknowledges Ambar's skills and
accomplishments.

AHMEDNAGAR

Chengiz Khan (Mirak Dabir) (d. 1574)—*Peshwa* of the Nizam Shahi who
mentors Ambar; Ambar names his second son after him.

Chand Bibi (1550–1599)—Daughter of Hussain Nizam Shah I, married to
Ali Adil Shah I of Bijapur. She served as Regent of Bijapur from
1580 to 1590 and Regent of Ahmednagar from 1596 to 1599 and
is best known for defending the Fort of Ahmednagar against the
Mughals in 1595. She is killed by her own troops who mistakenly
thought she was betraying the sultanate to the Mughals. Chand
means "moon."

Bibi Karima—Wife of Malik Ambar, referred to as a Siddi. She was a possible
confidante of his and was buried in a separate tomb near her
husband's.

Fateh Khan (Aziz Malik)—Eldest son of Malik Ambar; Fateh means
"victory."

Afzal Khan—Statesman and ambassador of Ahmednagar sent to negotiate
a truce with the Mughals in 1595 and then again by Shah Jahan
to Malik Ambar in 1623 for safety as the prince had decided to
revolt against his father.

Siddi Yakub Khan—An Abyssinian who was given the important charge
of commander-in-chief of the sultanate's cavalry and reported
directly to Malik Ambar, but eventually sides with Mughals.

Miyan Raju Dakhni (d. 1607)—Anti-Mughal rival in the Deccan;
imprisoned and killed in 1607.

Murtaza Nizam Shah I (r. 1565–1588)—Succeeds Hussein Nizam Shah
in 1565 and rules until 1588.

Burhan Nizam Shah II (r. 1591–1595)—His death in 1595 led to political
turmoil; he was the brother of Chand Bibi.

Murtaza Nizam Shah II (r. 1600–1610)—Malik Ambar places him on the
throne and has him poisoned.

Murtaza Nizam Shah III (r. 1633–1636)—Sultan of Ahmednagar from 1633
to 1636, may have been the brother of Fateh Khan's wife.

Maloji Raje Bhosale—Fought as a commander in Malik Ambar's army and led forces at the Battle of Bhatvadi in 1624. Shahaji Raje Bhosale (c. 1594–1664) was Maloji's son and also a commander in Malik Ambar's army and the father of Shivaji Bhosale (1627–1680)—the grandson of Maloji Raje Bhosale and great Maratha independence leader in the 1670s and 1680s.

Sant Tukaram (1608–1649)—Based in Dehu, near Puna, he was the Deccan's best-known Hindu poet.

BIJAPUR

Ikhlas Khan—Bijapuri Abyssinian noble originally named Malik Raihan; buried at Budaun, Uttar Pradesh.

Muhammed Qasim Ferishta (1560–1620)—Historian of the Deccan, formerly served as captain of the guards for the Nizam Shah, but wrote his *tarikh* in the Adil Shahi, from 1589 onwards. The history he wrote goes up to 1612.

Fuzuni Astarabadi—Author of *Fatuhat-i-Adil Shahi*, completed in 1643, which is the most comprehensive history of Malik Ambar from 1613 to 1626.

Ali Adil Shah I (r. 1558–1579)—Sultan of Bijapur, married to Chand Bibi. Installed his brother's son, Ibrahim, as his successor, since he himself did not have a son.

Ibrahim Adil Shah II (r. 1580/90–1627)—Long-time ruler of Bijapur who has a conflicted relationship with Malik Ambar.

Mulla Muhammad Lari—General who assisted Malik Ambar in 1616 but then commanded the imperial army in the Battle of Bhatvadi in 1624.

Hussain Nizam Shah I (r. 1553–1565)—Father of Chand Bibi.

EUROPEAN

Pieter van den Broecke (1585–1640)—Dutch trader and head of the Dutch East India Company (*Vereenigde Oostindische Compagnie*, or VOC) in the Deccan, who meets Malik Ambar in 1617 and provides a detailed account of his encounter.

Philip II (1527–1598)—King of Spain and Portugal who was interested in Ambar's relationship with the Mughals.

Pietro della Valle (1586–1652)—Italian nobleman and traveler who made
observations about Ambar in his *Viaggi*.

Francisco Álvares (c. 1465–c. 1541)—Portuguese priest who observed
the Ethiopian slave trade and offers a number of insights about
Abyssinia.

William Minor—Englishman who describes Malik Ambar's charity for the
poor in his account of the voyage of the *Scout*.

ACKNOWLEDGEMENTS

MY FATHER, ABU, A NATIVE of the Deccan and my favorite story-teller in the whole world, inspired me to write this book. He kindly and patiently read multiple drafts of the manuscript and commented at various points in the writing process with his always thoughtful insights, love, and humor. *Bahut shookira*, Abu.

The support of my family, friends, colleagues, and students has been vital in helping me produce these pages; most importantly, my darling *bivi*, Diana, and our cubs, Pablo and Samina, with whom life is so comforting, interesting, and fun; my mother, Lucy (Maria-Luz), who generously shared Abu with me while offering her own encouraging comments; my parents-in-law, Isabel y Jorge Munoz and my sister-in-law Caterine Munoz, whose homes in Girardot have been sanctuaries for writing during two summers, and, of course, my always protective and loving sister, Leslie, the *only* other East Indian-Peruvian-American I know; my best friends—and New York City crew—Chris Street, Carrie Sackett, and Cecilia Salvatierra, whose playfulness and *namak halal*, "fidelity to salt" (and sweets) is mutual; my friend Welansa Asrat; my brilliant colleague and friend Sylviane Diouf, whose creative and groundbreaking research in the African Diaspora never ceases to amaze me; my great professors Eric Foner and Maxwell Owusu, whose lessons I keep learning from; my wonderful colleagues and friends in Greensboro, including Frank Woods, Michael Cauthen, Sarah Cervenak, Bill Hart, Shelly Brown-Jeffy, George Dimock, Alyssa Gabbay, Abigail Browning, Asa Eger,

Vidya Gargeya, Edna Chun, Adrienne Middlebrooks, and Jamie Anderson, as well as my many current and former students, including Amanda Reams, Domonique Edwards, Khadija Sall, Charles Chavis, L'Erin Jensen, Almagul Kanafina, Stephanie Orosco, Yasmeen Chism, Adreanna Carter, Tiana Corbett, Ayah Khalifa, Lisa Seepaul, Tierra Moore, and sisters Sawsan and Nada Alnajjar, who inspire me in all the ways you do.

Several colleagues and friends in Ethiopia and India deserve special mention: Yikirta Alemu and Harya Yohannis, Professor Yohannes GebreMichael in the Department of Geography and Environmental Studies at Addis Ababa University, Professor Neeraj Salunkhe in the Department of History and Ancient Indian Culture at the Dr. B. Ambedkar Marathwada University in Aurangabad, and Blossom Medeira at the Goa Historical Archives—Directorate of Archives & Archeology. Other colleagues and friends who have helped me along the way include Robert Rook in the Department of History at Towson University, Ned Alpers in the Department of History at UCLA, Akbar Ahmed, the Ibn Khaldun Chair of Islamic Studies at American University, Issa Shivji, Professor of Law Emeritus at the University of Dar-es-Salaam, Abdul Sheriff, formerly of the Zanzibar Indian Ocean Research Institute and the Department of History and Archeology at the University of Dar-es-Salaam, and Navina Najat Haidar, curator of Islamic art at New York's Metropolitan Museum of Art, who offered critical insights and suggestions. I am indebted to each of you for your kindness and generosity of heart and mind over the years. Jyoti Gulati Balachandran, Colgate University, and Erik Gilbert, Arkansas State University, were commissioned by Oxford University Press to read a draft of the manuscript. I am grateful for their many instructive suggestions.

The work of historians is not possible without the careful work of librarians. Several librarians were especially helpful to me, including Gerald Holmes and Mark Schumacher of Jackson Library at The University of North Carolina at Greensboro, Hannah Rozear at Duke University's School of Divinity Library,

Sara Ann Sampson at UNC Chapel Hill's School of Law Library, and Karen Williams at the Thomas J. Watson Library of the Metropolitan Museum of Art in New York City. I have also benefited tremendously from the university library staffs of various Interlibrary Loan offices across the United States, including those at Columbia, Harvard, Princeton, Michigan, and the University of California, Berkeley.

Finally, a special thanks to OUP world history biography series editor Bonnie Smith, an extraordinary colleague whose elegance in prose and personality is unmatched, editorial assistant Lynn Luecken, product manager Leigh Ann Florek, copyeditor Wendy Walker, developmental production editor Lori Bradshaw, and executive editor Charles Cavaliere, who invited me to share this story with you through Oxford.

As Ambar would have whispered, *Alhamdulillah*.

ABOUT THE AUTHOR

OMAR H. ALI is Associate Professor of Comparative African Diaspora History and Interim Dean of Lloyd International Honors College at The University of North Carolina at Greensboro. A graduate of the London School of Economics and Political Science, he studied ethnography at the School of Oriental and African Studies before receiving his Ph.D. in History from Columbia University. He is the recipient of a Fulbright research award and a Teaching Excellence Award from The College of Arts & Sciences, where he helped to establish the Islamic Studies Research Network. In 2015 Ali was selected as the North Carolina Professor of the Year by The Carnegie Foundation for the Advancement of Teaching. Ali wrote the series of essays for the critically-acclaimed exhibit "The African Diaspora in the Indian Ocean World" for the Schomburg Center for Research in Black Culture (The New York Public Library), which was adopted by UNESCO as part of "The International Year for People of African Descent." He is the author of three other books, including, most recently, *Islam in the Indian Ocean World: A Brief History with Documents.* He has been a historical consultant to the Rockefeller Foundation, The College Board, The North Carolina Humanities Council, and the History Channel International, and has served on the Teaching Prize Committee of the World History Association. His multiple media appearances include CNN, PBS, NPR, and Al Jazeera.

INTRODUCTION

> In warfare, in command, in sound judgement, and in administration,
> he had no rival or equal . . . He kept down the turbulent spirits . . .
> maintained his exalted position to the end of his life, and closed
> his career in honour. History records no other instance of an
> Abyssinian slave arriving at such eminence.
>
> Mughal court chronicler Mu'tamad Khan
> *Tuzuk-i-Jahangiri*, Memoirs of Jahangir, 1627[1]

EVEN SOME OF MALIK AMBAR's greatest opponents would have to
acknowledge his multiple talents and accomplishments. Writing
soon after the death of the Mughal Emperor Jahangir—Ambar's
bitterest of enemies—the royal chronicler Mu'tamad Khan
seemed compelled to include the homage to the Deccani leader
in the Emperor's memoirs as if to set the historical record straight.
Both Jahangir and before him his father, the Emperor Akbar—
who referred to Ambar as "arrogant" and "evil-disposed"—found
it difficult to admit what was apparently well known: Ambar's exceptional military skills, governance, and administration. The
fact remained that despite their vast resources and powerful
armies, neither emperor was able to "conquer" the Deccan because of Ambar's relentless defense.

Forever frustrated, Jahangir described Ambar as "dark fate"
and "ill-starred," statements that seem to have been borne out
for him, the Emperor. (So obsessed did Jahangir become with
defeating Ambar that he even commissioned a fantasy painting
depicting him shooting arrows through his severed head impaled

1

on a spike.) However, other contemporaries—Deccanis, Europeans, and Mughals alike—had other words to describe Ambar. The Persian historian Muhammed Qasim Ferishta wrote of his "enterprising character and popularity"; the Dutch trader Pieter van den Broecke observed how "Melick keeps good order and laws in his country"; the distinguished Mughal emissary Asad Beg described Ambar as "a brave and discreet man"; and the Italian nobleman and traveler Pietro della Valle concluded, "This Malik Ambar is a man of great parts." In whichever light Ambar is portrayed, the historical record makes clear that he was an extraordinary figure.[2]

Ambar's career—his rise from slavery in East Africa to ruler in South Asia—sheds light on the diverse mix of people, products, and practices that shaped the Indian Ocean world during the early modern period (the fifteenth through eighteenth centuries). Originally from Ethiopia—historically called Abyssinia—Ambar is best known for having defended the Deccan from being occupied by the Mughals during the first quarter of the seventeenth century. His ingenuity as a military leader, his diplomatic skills, and his land reform policies contributed much to his success in keeping the Deccan free of Mughal imperial rule. Like the great Deccani political leader Chand Bibi, he engendered admiration, respect, and jealousy; and like her, his example inspired his generation and generations thereafter to fight for their independence.

Born in approximately 1548 in Hararghe in the eastern part of Ethiopia, where the highlands meet the lowlands, Ambar was ethnically Oromo—a pastoral and semi-agricultural people whose religious and spiritual practices included ancestral veneration, and whose social and political organization was based on the age-grade *Gadaa* system. Ambar was captured as a young person and sold into slavery and taken to southern Arabia in approximately 1560. From there he was traded and taken up to Baghdad. He converted to Islam and was subsequently educated while in the service of Mir Qasim, a Baghdadi merchant who took him to India.

Around 1571 Ambar was sold in western India to the Abyssinian statesman Mirak Dabir, more widely known as Chengiz Khan. Khan, who had once been a slave himself, was now the prime minister (*peshwa*) of the Nizam Shah—the Sultan of Ahmednagar in the northwestern part of the Deccan (one of the five kingdoms in the region). Khan spent several years mentoring Ambar in the ways of the court and the military but was murdered in 1574. Leaving Ahmednagar after being freed by Khan's widow, Ambar led a small cavalry force, serving as a mercenary in neighboring Bijapur as part of the thousands of African slave-soldiers and mercenaries who were in demand among Indian monarchs at the time.

In 1595 Ambar returned to the Ahmednagar Sultanate to help protect its capital and main fort against Mughal attack before dispersing into the countryside and continuing to build his own following. At the turn of the seventeenth century Ambar, now with a sizable army under his command, made himself Regent on behalf of a young royal member of the family he installed as Nizam Shah. Ambar later placed another young heir onto the Nizam Shahi throne, continuing to serve as *de facto* ruler until his death in 1626 at the age of approximately eighty.

Not only was Ambar a skilled diplomat, administrator, and military strategist—whose name was known to emperors, princes, and peasants alike—but he also developed a highly effective form of guerilla warfare, *bargi-giri*, which employed quick-striking Maratha light cavalry. Ambar strengthened Ahmednagar's existing fortifications; created an innovative land revenue system that increased agricultural productivity; designed and built a model capital, Khirki (Fatehnagar), with palaces, mosques, and an extensive water supply system (the *Nahr*); maximized the flow of trade in his realm; and patronized Muslim and Hindu artisans, adding to the unique artistry of the region. Most famously, however, and for over a quarter-century, Ambar defended the Deccan against Mughal incursions—at times conceding territory to the northern imperialists, but then turning around and pushing them out.

Malik Ambar portrait by the artist Hashim, circa 1624, Ahmednagar.

The following biography is based on late sixteenth- and early seventeenth-century Persian, Urdu, Marathi, Dutch, English, Italian, Spanish, and Portuguese documents, including royal chronicles, letters, and administrative records, as well as oral history, paintings, monuments, and the remains of structures that stand or once stood in the Deccan. Among the most detailed and illuminating written sources on Ambar are those by the Deccani-based Persian historian Muhammed Qasim Ferishta (*Tarikh-i-Ferishta*, completed in 1612), the Dutch merchant Pieter van den Broecke (the account of his meeting with Ambar in 1617), and the Bijapuri court chronicler Fuzuni Astarabadi (*Fatuhat-i-Adil Shah*, completed in 1643). Synthesizing much of the existing scholarship on Ambar's life and times, the biography builds on the research of Jogindra Nath Chowdhuri (1933), Banarasi P. Saksena (1941), Radhey Shyam (1968), Bhaskar G. Tamaskar (1978), Shanti Sadiq Ali (1996), Ababu Minda Yimene (2004), Richard M. Eaton (2005), and Klaus Rotzer (2006).

My own research took me from Ethiopia to India and included work in local and national archives, ethnographic fieldwork, and archeological study. From the area of Ambar's birthplace in central Ethiopia, I traveled to India's Konkan Coast and up the western Ghats to Puna, a major thoroughfare of Ambar's Ahmednagar; Bijapur, where Ambar served during Bibi's Regency; Sholapur, one of several cities in the western Deccan whose fort he "took by storm"; Khirki, the model city he built and rebuilt (renamed Aurangabad); Daulattabad, Ambar's third capital and site of one of the most impenetrable forts in the Deccan; Ambarpur, near the sacred village of Khuldabad, where he constructed his *dargah* (tomb); and along the byways and open fields, the hills, and the riverbanks of the Deccan, where Ambar's agricultural reforms improved the lives of the largely voiceless peasants of the region—the subaltern of the early modern period, those who worked the land and produced the food that fed the monarchs, *amirs* (nobles), and armies, and on whose backs lay the heaviest burden of war.

In the following account of Ambar's life and times, I draw attention to the African presence in the Deccan, long-distance cultural diffusion, issues of gender and race, the institution of military slavery, and the interplay between social and imperial history. A number of scholars have led the way in my understanding of Ambar's life, Shyam, Tamaskar, and Eaton being my most valuable guides. I am most indebted to them for their pioneering and perceptive work. In addition to the text, included are several maps, paintings, and excerpts of primary sources to help orient the reader and help deepen Malik Ambar's story, the world that shaped his actions, and whose actions, in turn, shaped the world in which he lived.

CHAPTER 1

| OROMO, ABYSSINIA, AND WAR |

THE FIGHTING WAS INCESSANT. Born and bred in the midst of war, the Oromo's youngest generation knew little of life beyond the battles that raged around them—that is, the time before the great migration. With an expanding population in search of land, the Oromo—a decentralized, pastoral, and semi-agricultural people—began migrating from southern into central Ethiopia in the 1530s. Battling first the imperial Ethiopian Christians and then the Ethiopian Muslims of the Adal Sultanate, the Oromo had transformed themselves. Like their Christian and Muslim counterparts, they learned to fight on horseback. Now, they too would take captives, whom they exchanged for food, arms, and supplies—the spoils and consequences of war.[1]

It was into this war-torn context that Chapu, an Oromo, later dubbed Malik Ambar, breathed his first breath. Chapu's mother gave birth to him in approximately 1548 in the area of Hararghe. Located in central-east Ethiopia, Hararghe's cool and rugged plateaus fall into shallow, sometimes steep valleys. There, in one of those valleys, a young Oromo mother might have sat next to one of a thousand campfires reflecting the stars above. Gazing down at her infant son's profile flickering in the light, she may have thought, soon, he too would be clapping along to the *helee* songs that had once been sung to her in what was only a clap and yet a lifetime ago.[2]

Although there is little documentary evidence about Ambar's
childhood, there are multiple references of him being called
Chapu, with variations of the name being used throughout his
life—as in, "Ambar Jiū," appearing in both Mughal and Adil Shah
court records.[3] The name is either a reference to his family's
southern Kambaata origins or derived from *shaambisa*, meaning "fertility" or "growth" in Afaan Oromoo, the language of his
people. In this way, the name may have reflected his family's
memory of a distant homeland *or* their hopes for a better future—
perhaps both.[4] Many years later, while living in Baghdad, his
then-owner Mir Qasim renamed him Ambar (either the precious
stone or in Arabic *ambar*: "ambergris"); years thereafter, his
then-sponsor, the Sultan of Bijapur in India, gave him the honorific title Malik ("king" in Arabic, or "chief"), completing what
he would become variously known as: Malik Ambar, a powerful
name befitting the extraordinary life he would come to lead.

The details of how Ambar was initially enslaved are debat-
able. Early in his youth, however, he was taken from his family
and forced into the flow of humanity feeding Ethiopia's slave
markets—at Gondar, Gallabar, Massawa, and Zeila, among
others. Every year, thousands of Abyssinians were captured, enslaved, and taken to various parts of the Middle East and the
wider Indian Ocean world. Commenting in 1555 on the robust
slave trade, the Portuguese priest Gonçalo Rodrigues reported
that every year "more than ten or twelve thousand slaves" were
captured and sold in Ethiopia.[5]

War and the slave trade ravaged the Oromo, as it would other
people and their communities, even as many—including Oromo—
thrived as a result of it. Captives were taken up to Cairo and into
the heart of the Ottoman Empire; others were taken to Arabia,
Persia, India, and Ceylon (Sri Lanka). In India they would be
called "Habshi"—derived from the Arabic *Habasha* for Abyssinia,
the ancient name for Ethiopia—which comprised people from
not only the hinterlands of Ethiopia but also Somalia and the
Sudan. They were later called "Siddi"—possibly derived from

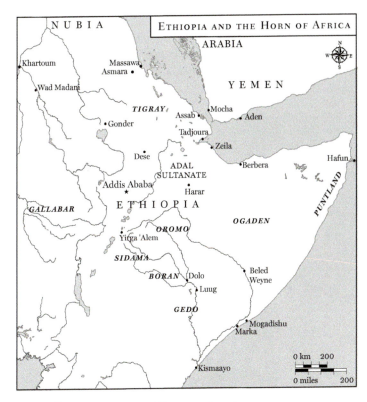

MAP 1. Ethiopia and the Horn of Africa

saydi, "captive" in Arabic, or *sayyid*, an honorific title used in Arabic, originally to denote someone in the lineage of the Prophet Muhammad (possibly picked up in reference to the Arab captains referred to as such who initially brought Africans to the area of Iran/Pakistan). These Africans served in a number of capacities—including as concubines and domestic servants, in the case of women; and as soldiers and guards, in the case of men.[6] Dehumanized but never fully stripped of their humanity, Habshi women were renowned for their beauty among Arab and Persian chroniclers, Habshi men for their wit and bravery—descriptions as much as justifications for their enslavement.

Abyssinian warriors, either slave soldiers or mercenaries, served monarchs and merchants of every background and faith across the western Indian Ocean world. For centuries Habshis made up the ranks of Muslim Arab armies, as they did the crews of Arab,

Abyssinian warriors.

Persian, and Indian merchant ships.[7] As the traveler and Muslim jurist Ibn Battuta described from personal experience, Abyssinians were long regarded as "the guarantors of safety on [the Indian Ocean] . . . let there be but one of them on a ship and it will be avoided by the Indian pirates and idolaters."[8]

In Ambar's sixteenth-century Abyssinia, the cycle of violence continued, with war producing captives, which in turn produced more war. The Oromo along with other peoples from across the Indian Ocean world—from the smallest decentralized polities to those in or on the edges of massive imperial stretches—seemed locked in interminable conflict during the period to protect or expand their boundaries or their spheres of political and economic influence, namely access to trade routes. Ambar's Abyssinia had long been characterized by a constellation of political forces. Over time, however, a sharp political divide emerged that saw the rise of the Ethiopian Christian empire ruling over much of the country's non-Christian peasant farmers and herdsmen. As early as the fourth century C.E., the Ethiopian Orthodox Tewahedo Church, whose emperors considered themselves the descendants of King Solomon, had become the state's religion. Under the empire's authority, subjects in both the highlands and in much of the lowlands paid taxes through the *gult* revenue system; payment was taken in the form of grain or cattle, sometimes honey and butter, or by subjects providing their labor.

Overseeing the various lands were governors who reported to Aksum, the seat of the ancient kingdom of the same name that ruled the northern part of the country and extended its authority across the Red Sea to southwestern Arabia. Although Aksum served as the imperial capital for part of the early modern period, in Ambar's era Ethiopia's emperors moved regularly, as various state affairs compelled them to travel throughout the country. Their shifting capital sometimes numbered in the tens of thousands. One impressed Portuguese missionary, Father Francisco Álvares, described one sprawling imperial encampment as "a city in a great plain," filled with colorful pavilions, markets, and military barracks.[9]

To the east of the highlands were the lowlands, stretching to the Red Sea and Gulf of Aden ports of Massawa and Zeila. With the spread of Islam along the region's trade routes, Muslim merchants had come to dominate much of the coastline, and parts of the interior. The lowlands, with dozens of small polities, included the large commercial center Harar, a Muslim walled city at the footsteps of the highlands within the Hararghe region. Not only was Harar a crossroads linking the people and products of the eastern ports to the products and people of the towns and cities in the west, but its wealth generated significant patronage for Muslim scholars, making it the foremost center of Islamic learning on the Horn of Africa, indeed all of eastern Africa south of Egypt.

Rivaling the Christian and Muslim Abyssinian populations living in the lowlands were Ambar's people in eastern and western Ethiopia. They practiced their own forms of spirituality, including ancestral veneration, however the Oromo's creator-god *Waaqa tokkicha* ("the one God") was not so different from either the Judeo-Christian or Muslim God: the source of all life, omniscient, omnipresent, and omnipotent. The Oromo's monotheism likely predated, and may have even influenced, the Judeo-Christian-Muslim traditions—from the Lower Nile, through Nubia, down the Upper Nile to Egypt, over to the Levant, and down to Arabia.[10] Despite being at war, Abyssinian Christians, Muslims, and Oromo therefore shared much of the same basic religious understanding of creation and spiritual life. Among these multiple peoples, the Oromo were also the largest ethnic group among a number of Abyssinian peoples, a decentralized nation unto themselves.

Throughout Ambar's youth Muslim Abyssinians variously challenged imperial Ethiopian Christian rule. A generation before his birth, starting in 1527, the Adal Sultanate of eastern Ethiopia launched a *jihad* against the Christian empire. They were joined by their Portuguese co-religionists. The war between the Muslim and Christian forces lasted for over fourteen years and boosted the slave trade, with captives coming from all sides. The defeat of the Adal Sultanate in 1543, with the aid of Portuguese troops and firepower, was soon followed by an effort by the Amirate of Harar to reclaim authority over the now-beleaguered city. Beginning in the 1550s and continuing through the 1560s—that is, during Ambar's youth—the Amirate of Harar waged war not only against the Christians but also against the Oromo, who had been steadily advancing into the area of Hararghe in central Ethiopia.[11]

Still, life continued in the midst of war: Children were born, people created families, and communities were made. Despite the violence, and its consequences—death, injuries, dislocation, hunger, thirst, emotional pain, and the social impact on everyone involved—people also sang, laughed, told stories, and comforted each other. The world into which Ambar was born was therefore one of contrasts, of attacks and counterattacks, battles and more battles, and of tenderness in the mix—a world that paralleled the embattled people of the Deccan throughout the same period in a number of ways, of those who sustained the lives of those around them as destruction stormed through their fields, their homes, and their communities. Abyssinia foreshadowed much of what Ambar would encounter in India: imperial expansion and anti-imperial resistance, contested local political authority, military retooling, alliance making, cultural and religious diffusion, broken treaties, the pride of the people, and the burden of war.

Although many traditions prevailed during Ambar's early childhood, profound social transformations were also under way. Much of Oromo social and political organization had been based on their *Gadaa* system with age-grade classes (*luba*) that succeeded each other every eight years. The new leaders of the society assumed military, political, and economic responsibilities for the community as a whole. While the Oromo fought routinely—in fact, a prerequisite for the transfer of power every eight years entailed that the aspiring new leaders prove themselves through battle—they, unlike Christian or Muslim Abyssinians, adopted their captured enemies in groups called *mogaasa* as equal members of their society. This kind of assimilation of captives into

Oromo society generally led to more humane treatment than the captives of Christians or Muslims, who, in sharp contrast, separated family members as part of their slave trading.[12] The combination of migration and war in the sixteenth century, however, changed Oromo societies as they encountered new people, environments, and political conditions.

Oromo reactions and calculated responses to the challenges of war and shifting material conditions led some groups to take radical steps. Some Oromo groups, including the Yahabattas, Iima Gwozit, and Talatas, formed alliances with the Christian empire and converted to their religion; others became major slave traders.[13] Oromo conversions to both Christianity and Islam began to increase throughout the period. In turn, unconverted Oromo chiefs began supplying Christian Oromo captives to Muslim markets to acquire arms, supplies, and horses—allowing for greater protection against raids and the ability to go on the offensive. The result was a significant increase in slave trading among all Oromo groups—Muslims, animists, and Christians alike—whose facial marks could sometimes identify their loyalties. For instance, the sixteenth-century Portuguese traveler Tomé Pires noted that enslaved Christian Oromo could be recognized by the cross-shaped branding on their foreheads (a practice that replaced baptism).[14] For many Oromo embracing the slave trade was a survival strategy, necessary to protect immediate kin and community, even if it increased overall enslavement and slave trading—including that of other Oromo.

Oromo were among the largest number of Abyssinian captives, regularly filling the markets at Gondar and Gallabar in northwestern Ethiopia. Christian-ruled Gondar, located just north of Tana Lake, lay at the intersection of three major caravan routes: one running south across the Blue Nile and into the southwest—a principal source of gold, ivory, and captives; while the other two trade routes ran northeast to the port of Massawa and northwest to Sudan, continuing up to Egypt.[15] While Christian Abyssinians controlled these northern centers of commerce, Muslim merchants were its principal traders. All Oromo, however, were brought into the trade. By the mid-sixteenth century Christian and non-Christian Oromo were regularly engaging in slave raiding and trading. Ambar, as a child, was likely a witness to such raiding and counter-raiding. As chroniclers record, thousands of Oromo were caught in the crosscurrents of war and trade; upwards of five hundred Oromo were sold at Gallabar in a single day. From Gallabar, among other slave markets, captives were sold to points even farther north and to the east.[16]

Although Ambar's particular circumstances upon capture have not been recorded, some of his family must have been around him when he was taken into captivity. Were they also captured? Several historians claim (without supporting evidence) that his parents sold him into slavery due to poverty, but it is equally possible that he was seized in the course of war.[17] However, without written records or recorded oral history, the circumstances of Ambar's enslavement remain speculative. Along these lines, who were his parents? Were they leaders in his Oromo community or ordinary subjects? Did Ambar have siblings? And if so, what happened to them?

The historical record is silent on such specifics. However, we do know that female captives were subject to sexual assault—preyed upon, harassed, even raped—by their owners, although boys were also known to have been exploited in these ways. One author has stated that Oromo women "were sought for their commonly slim shape, regular features, celebrated gazelle-like eyes, and long, straight, or slightly curled hair. Market convention ascribed particular beauty to Oromo girls and peculiar intelligence to Oromo boys."[18] Such descriptions, however, belie the violence of slavery—a system based on the threat and regular use of force.[19]

Being a male captive in Muslim societies had certain relative advantages over being a female captive, which was expressed in Islamic conventions. Within Muslim societies many of the

Ethiopian slave caravan.

younger males purchased by sultans, princes, or wealthy families were provided with a level of education by their masters that could lead them to gaining significant authority in their own right—as managers of finances, workforce supervisors, military commanders, and political advisors.[20] Ambar's future might therefore entail a degree of upward social mobility. However, in order for opportunities to open up, Ambar would need to be purchased by someone with sufficient wealth, position, and sense; someone who could see Ambar's particular values and traits— his "peculiar intelligence"—and decide to invest in his advanced training and education. At this point Ambar would not have been aware of such possibilities. In the days, weeks, and months following his captivity, other feelings and thoughts would have likely consumed him: shock, confusion, fright, anger, his family.

Perhaps standing at the port of Zeila alongside dozens of other captives, sometime around 1560, Ambar would have been able to taste the salt in the air as the breeze pushed the sea inland.

One can imagine Ambar, Chapu, still a boy, looking at the various boats—*sambuq, mtepe,* and *dhow*—approaching and leaving the Gulf of Aden at the point where the land meets the sea, and for captives, the point of no return. His journey was well under way. From Hararghe to Zeila he would have had to walk over two hundred miles across one of the hottest stretches of land on Earth to reach the coast.[21] Shortly after arriving at the port of Zeila he would have been bartered or sold for rock salt, pieces of cloth, or thin bars of iron—the various currencies of the area—along with the coffee beans, musk, ivory, silk, and other products and commodities that were being traded across the region at the time. The conversations he had, the thoughts that ran through his mind, the tears he shed, and the things he saw on the long route from the Abyssinian foothills to the coast remain his own.

Closing his eyes, the young Oromo would have also been able to pick out the familiar sounds and rhythms of his language amid the cacophony of other languages that swirled around him, including Arabic, Hadiyya, Gujarati, Somali, and Afar. As with the many thousands of other children abruptly taken from their families, Chapu would need to grow up quickly. His destiny now lay somewhere beyond the horizon, somewhere else. Stepping into a small, unsteady vessel, the young Ambar braced himself as he was about to leave his family's land, their heart, and his former life, forever.[22]

CHAPTER 2

MOCHA, BAGHDAD, AND BEYOND

MOCHA, A BUSTLING PORT CITY on the Arabian side of the Red Sea, was an *entrepôt* for a range of commodities coming in and out of East Africa: locally produced frankincense, myrrh, and coffee from Yemen; cotton and spices from India, long in demand in Ethiopia; dates from Oman to celebrate the breaking of the fast during the Muslim month of Ramadan; gold and ivory from Africa's interior—the latter prized as far away as China for its strength and color; mangrove poles from the Swahili coast for the construction of houses, palaces, and mosques; and, of course, captives, to be trained and used as domestic servants, concubines, construction workers, administrators, guards, and soldiers.

Malik Ambar was sold to an Arab merchant at Mocha for twenty ducats, a gold-based currency used across much of the Ottoman Empire—which, by the end of the sixteenth century, stretched from Anatolia down to the southern tip of Arabia.[1] Twenty ducats was most likely a fair market price for a young, un-trained, Oromo captive, who would also require clothing, food, and seasoning—additional investments that an owner would need to make. From the standpoint of the captive, however, fairness did not characterize their enslavement—even though slavery was viewed in this period as a natural part of virtually all societies.

From Zeila, Ambar would have traveled through the strait of *Bab-al-Mandib*—the "Gate of Grief"—passing the Sawabi Islands to reach Mocha on the other side of the narrow body of water connecting the Gulf of Aden to the Red Sea. In Mocha, where Ambar may have stayed for weeks, perhaps months, mingling with other captives and taking whatever orders from his captor, he would have also taken in the aromas of local dishes spiced with red chilies from Aden, or eaten *malooga*, a popular Yemeni flatbread. Ambar was now in Arab country, with its own language, cultures, and customs, which he would observe and perhaps begin to emulate—if only as a way to better negotiate the various challenges he must have faced in his new environment.

A merchant named Kazi Hussein purchased Ambar. Nothing is known of this trader except that his name suggests he may have been Shi'a, as opposed to Sunni—the dominant branch of Islam.[2] From Mocha Ambar either was taken north, up the Arabian coast, and would have stopped at the port of Jeddah—the point of entry for Ethiopian, Sudanese, and other African pilgrims going to Mecca—or sailed east around Aden, along the southwestern coast of Arabia (Yemen's Hadhramaut) to Muscat in Oman, and then up the Persian Gulf to Basra in southern Iraq, and on to Baghdad via the Tigris River. If he traveled up the western coast of Arabia to Mecca he would have soon found himself immersed among the masses heading toward the spiritual center of the Muslim world.

Throughout the sixteenth century, tens of thousands of pilgrims traveled to Mecca to perform the Hajj—the pilgrimage that Muslims strive to complete at least once in their lifetime. Pilgrims traveled by caravan and by sea, arriving from across the entire *ummah* (Muslim community): from West Africa and the Maghreb to China and Southeast Asia, from the imperial capitals of Istanbul, Cairo, Baghdad, Isfahan, and Delhi, to hamlets and villages on the Swahili, Hadhramaut, Makran, and Malabar coasts. Pilgrims included rich and poor, rulers and ruled.

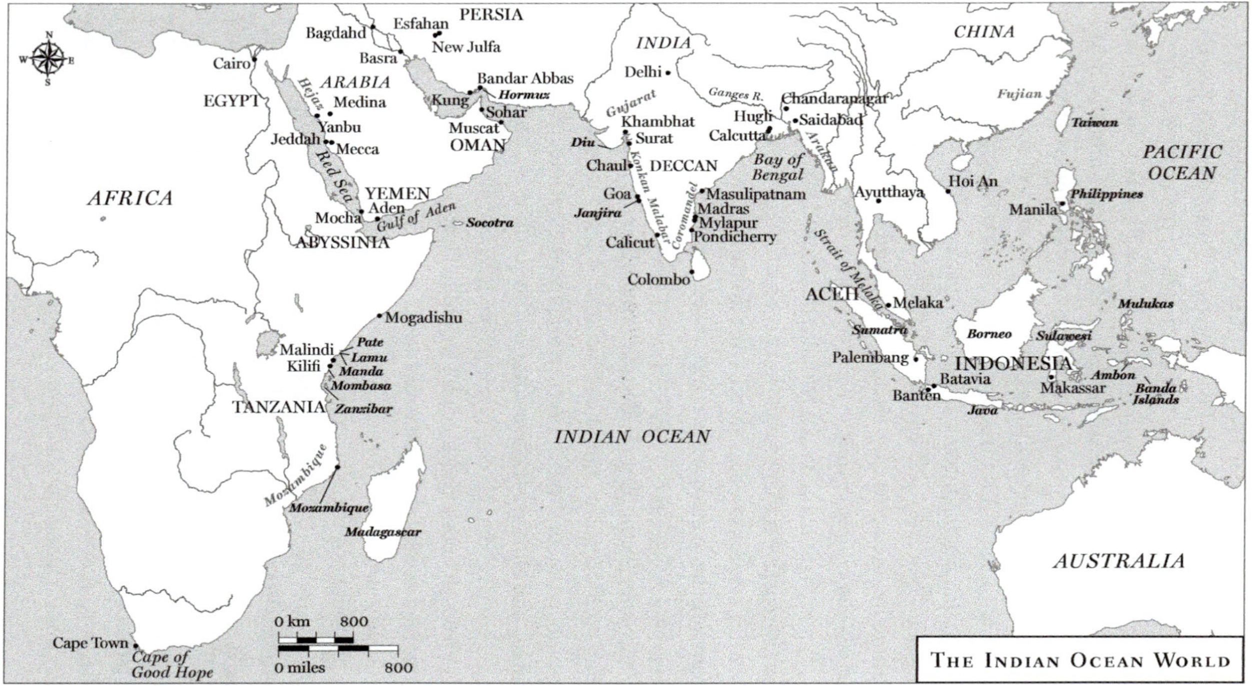

MAP 2. The Indian Ocean World

Every year as part of the Hajj, sultans, nobles, Sufis, scholars, and students headed toward Mecca, and always with traders in tow. While most pilgrims made the journey with great sacrifice, often with the financial assistance of their communities and at significant risk (ever-possible attack of caravan raiders and pirates), a few traveled in extraordinary luxury and security. Most famously, two centuries before Ambar's journey from Africa to Arabia, Mansa Musa, the West African emperor of Mali, traveled to Mecca with an entourage of sixty thousand people—including thousands of servants and slaves, with drums beating, horns blaring, and elephants and camels laden with gold. The vast majority of pilgrims, however, were ordinary people—including people such as Ambar's traders—who made the journey to western Arabia.[3]

At some point between Mocha and Baghdad, Ambar either decided to adopt Islam on his own or was encouraged by his master to do so. Whether he assumed a Muslim identity at the time as an act of genuine faith or simply as a practical matter of assimilation is not known. Either way, he would have quickly learned the benefits of conversion to Islam in a predominantly Muslim world. Conversion would have entailed Ambar making the *shahada*, the declaration of faith in Arabic: *La ilaha illa-Allah Muhamadur Rasulullah* ("There is only one God, and Muhammad is his Messenger"). Beyond this, being a Muslim would also require Ambar to perform daily prayer and maintain certain dietary restrictions (no pork, no alcohol)—among other things. Muslims, like those of other faiths, however, ranged significantly in their religious practice. For Ambar, an indication of his own genuine faith in Islam may be glimpsed by the fact that decades later he would personally instruct his soldiers in the Qur'an. As a boy and adolescent, though, his conversion to Islam was likely a matter of course.[4]

Had Ambar gone up the Red Sea route, he would have landed at the port of Jeddah. Here, Ambar would have been approaching sacred land. It was here, in this western area of Arabia—the Hejaz—that the Muslim community had initially formed. The

Hejaz was home to two of its holiest cities, Mecca and Medina. Tens of thousands of pilgrims annually passed through the port of Jeddah on their way to performing the Hajj (or the *Umrah*, the pilgrimage outside of the prescribed time in the year to be considered a proper "Hajji"). In addition to being the location of the Ka'aba, the ancient site of worship, Mecca was home to many Ethiopians, perhaps the best known being Bilal Ibn Rabah. A close companion of the Prophet Muhammad during the early seventh century, Bilal was a former slave who started the Islamic tradition of the call to prayer, the *azzan*, heard daily across the Muslim world.[5]

At some point during his youth in the early mornings and evenings, Ambar may have heard the *azzan* in the distance. Being in the area of Harar, the *azzan* was never too far. At the Muslim ports of Zeila and Mocha, Ambar would have certainly heard the call to prayer—with its opening powerful proclamation, *"Allah-u-Akbar"* ("God is greatest"). In the Hejaz Ambar would have been near the source of the *azzan*. Mecca lies just to the east of Jeddah in a narrow valley about one thousand feet above sea level. Whether or not Ambar joined his latest owner in Mecca is not known. At some point, however, had he *not* traveled the southern sea route around the Arabian Peninsula up the Persian Gulf to the port of Basra and then up the Tigris to Baghdad, he would have joined a caravan heading toward Baghdad, then under Ottoman imperial rule.

Baghdad-bound caravans were like long, slow-moving towns winding through the desert at night. Traveling largely after sundown to avoid the scorching heat of the day, such caravans were highly organized. The largest caravans, from Cairo, Damascus, and Baghdad, enjoyed state support, including imperial guards, provisions, and attention to the poor. As Ibn Battuta described in his own journey from Mecca to Baghdad during the fourteenth century, "whenever the caravan halted, food was cooked in great brass cauldrons, and from these the needs of the poorer pilgrims and those who had no provisions were supplied . . . the caravan included busy *bazaars* and many commodities, as well as all sorts of food and fruit. They used to march during the night and light torches in front of the file of camels . . . so that you saw the countryside gleaming with light and the darkness turned into radiant day."[6] Ambar may have joined a caravan of this kind from Mecca to Baghdad with returning pilgrims and merchants—although by the sixteenth century most pilgrims from Baghdad preferred the longer, safer route via Damascus.

Baghdad, the former capital of the Abbasid Caliphate, whose court of Harun al-Rashid served as the basis of *The Arabian Nights*, was the largest city Ambar would see in his lifetime. Ahmednagar, for a time the seat of Ambar's Deccani sultanate, was at its height compared to Baghdad in its design and architecture—albeit on a smaller scale. Sprawling with nearly half a million inhabitants, few other cities at the time rivaled Baghdad in size, even as it was centuries past its golden age. Falling under Ottoman rule, Baghdad remained an iconic metropolis of the Muslim world. Other cities, notably Cairo, Istanbul, and Delhi, had surpassed it in terms of population, and as centers of intellectual and artistic development, yet Baghdad held its place among the world's great cities, having boasted the *Bayt al-Hikma* ("House of Wisdom")—a library that brought together scholars, translators, and copyists working on synthesizing scientific knowledge from ancient Greece, Egypt, Persia, India, and China.

The great city's mix of Arab and Persian culture, art, and architectural design inspired Muslims, including Ambar, as well as non-Muslims across the world. Baghdad's Arab and Persian designs were markers of urban sophistication, mixing geometric and florid patterns, vaulted entrances, arches, domes, calligraphic inscriptions, and sleek surfaces and lines. Such artistic and architectural designs would become part of Ambar's own aesthetic, which he brought with him to the Deccan, as seen in the palaces, mosques, and tombs that he would later build.[7]

Getting to Baghdad from Mecca was no small feat. For slaves and the poor, the long desert journey up the Hejaz and over the

Peninsula was harsh. Despite the attention of caravan organizers to the poor, as a slave, Ambar would have been given the fewest amenities in terms of food and water, but enough to survive the 1,200 miles he would have walked had he taken this route. Passing through the oasis town of Tayma, pilgrims, traders, and servants would have quenched their thirst by drinking from the well of Haddaj, or eaten the olives and dates that grew near the wells at Al-Jawaf, another oasis town en route.

Finally reaching Baghdad's gates sometime in the early 1560s, Ambar would have been amazed at what he saw—the sheer size of the city, its exquisite architecture, gardens, fountains, shaded walkways, and covered bazaars. Even before reaching the city limits, he would have seen the multiple minarets punctuating Baghdad's skyline. Among the hundreds of thousands of people living in the city were other Abyssinians—many of whom were free. Indeed, long before Ambar's arrival to Baghdad, another Abyssinian, Al-Jahiz, the grandson of Ethiopians, was his generation's leading person of letters. In one of his most famous books, *Kitab Fakhr As-Sudan 'Ala Al-Bidan* ("The Book of Pride of the Blacks over the Whites"), he describes Ethiopians as "more eloquent than a wisp of smoke."[8] He writes of the talents, beauty, and accomplishments of Nubians (Upper Nilotic Egyptians and Sudanese) and Habshi (Abyssinians and Somali) who "filled [Arab lands] amply through marriage, chieftainship and lordship, and have been used . . . for protection from your enemies."[9] Africans had apparently been a visible presence throughout the region and especially valued as safe keepers and protectors—a tradition earlier noted by Ibn Battuta and one that Ambar would continue.

Ambar was next purchased in Baghdad—this time by a *qadi* of Mecca, Qazi-ul-Quzat. Quzat may have been trying to turn a quick profit, as it appears that he soon sold Ambar to another merchant, Khwaja Mir Baghdadi, better known as Mir Qasim. Ambar's latest owner was from Baghdad (as his name Baghdadi suggests) and apparently treated his young Abyssinian slave—at least according to one interpretation—"like his own son with utmost generosity and kindness."[10] Qasim was chiefly responsible for Ambar's early education. Here was an owner that could and would open up doors for him.

Ambar's education under Qasim's tutelage included reading, writing as well as basic finance, skills that would make him more valuable and serve him well in time. Being in Baghdad was an education in and of itself. Ambar spent a number of formative years in the city, where he internalized the culture, sensibilities, and tastes of the cosmopolitan life. He learned Arabic—as any educated Muslim would—and perhaps some Persian, the language of some of Islam's most celebrated poetry, from Omar Khayyam to Jalal ad-Din Rumi, in addition to "Arabic lore and literature."[11]

Ambar would have been exposed to a range of people in Baghdad—those living there and those who came through the city on business, for pleasure, or a combination of reasons. Most likely, as a trusted and educated slave, Ambar would have also traveled with Mir Qasim on business. In this way, his circles of contact probably shifted over time from fellow servants to heads of households, guests, and businessmen, even as he may have found himself gravitating towards other Abyssinians in the urban center. Eventually, though, the paternalistic relationship (if that was indeed the case) between his master and himself came to an end. The bottom line was never in dispute: Ambar was property—not an heir nor a son, but a slave.

Whether to make a profit or to offer his young assistant new opportunities—perhaps both—Mir Qasim decided to take his now twenty-something-year-old to India. Leaving Baghdad around 1571, Ambar would have traveled down the Tigris River to the port of Basra, *Sindbad*'s home. Located at the head of the Persian Gulf on the *Shatt al-Arab*—the "stream of the Arabs"—where the Tigris and Euphrates meet, Basra was the former site of the Zanj Revolt, a massive slave uprising in lower Iraq from 869 to 883. It was the largest insurrection of slaves in world history—that is, until the Haitian Revolution of 1791, a thousand years later, and on the other side of the world. Meticulously documented by the Arab historian al-Tabari, the Zanj Revolt was multiracial and included black military leaders such as al-Zanji b. Mihran, who commanded the flow of arms up and down the great twin rivers of Mesopotamia. Defeated after fourteen years of war, the rebellion shook the very foundations of the Abbasid Caliphate, arguably helping to lead to its imperial downfall. However, all of this would have been a distant memory to the people of Basra by the time Ambar meandered through the city's waterfront market accompanying his master.

The next leg of Ambar's journey would have entailed traveling the length of the Persian Gulf to reach the Arabian Sea. Upon entering the waters of the Gulf, one might hear Muslim travelers uttering "*Alhamdulillah*" (thanks and praise to God)—an iteration of comfort and gratitude sounded across the *ummah*. While the Gulf waters permitted free sailing (unlike the Red Sea, with its dangerous shoals) it had its own perils, especially for pearl-diving slaves—one of dozens of types of slaves across the Indian Ocean world. The long, repeated plunges into the depths of the Gulf by these slaves were often fatal. Swimming head-first down to 100 feet with pouches strapped on to their bodies, pearl divers regularly sustained eye damage and blackouts from cerebral hypoxia before succumbing to their ends. Like other slave-produced goods in the region—from salt collected from evaporating pools of seawater to dates picked on the plantations of the region—each pearl had its own hidden story, its own human cost.

A two-and-a-half-day's journey south would have landed Ambar and his master at the Persian port of Gamrun (Bandar Abbas) at the buckle of the Gulf's Strait of Hormuz. After picking up fresh supplies and perhaps switching boats and *nakhudas* ("captains" in Persian), their journey would have continued toward the Arabian Sea—the *Sindhu Sagar* ("Sea of Sind" in Sanskrit), as Hindus called it. Never traveling too far from the Makran coast of the northern Arabian Sea, Ambar and Mir Qasim would have finally reached western India's Konkan coast just over a fortnight after leaving Baghdad.

Having made it this far by sea was an achievement in and of itself. As the thirteenth-century Arab traveler Ibn al-Mujawir noted in his journal, "A man's return from the sea is like his rise from the grave, and the port is like the place of congregation on the Day of Judgment: there is questioning [and] settlement of accounts." Ambar's journey, however, was a one-way trip for which he was himself to be settled, but it was no less dangerous, despite centuries-old travel across the Arabian Sea. The sea, with its powerful currents and winds, could, and would, unleash its fury at a moment's notice. In addition to hurricanes and sudden storms, travelers faced the threat of pirates, including coordinated multi-ship assaults that entrapped even the most experienced of navigators.[12]

As fortune or fate would have it, Ambar made it safely in the early 1570s from Baghdad to the western coast of India, whose ports served as a nexus of international trade. Ambar most likely landed first at the Gujarati port of Surat, a key *entrepôt* of the western Indian Ocean, before continuing on to Chaul farther south. Surat, like Chaul, brought a panoply of people and products, including Muslim pilgrims, pepper, and Chinese porcelain from as far away as Aceh in northern Sumatra to ivory and gold from Mombasa on the Swahili coast.[13] Ambar seems to have arrived at Chaul just as it was being rebuilt following the Nizam Shahi's destructive siege that wrested it from Portuguese control. The port quickly became the sultanate's most important and prosperous holding on the coast, trading an array of specialized goods, including diamonds from Golconda, Kashmiri shawls, Japanese silks, amber and "fragrant substances" from Zanzibar, and military slaves from Abyssinia. The Englishman Thomas Nicolls would describe Chaul in the early sixteenth century as "extremely prosperous and famous for its imports."[14]

Ambar would later return to Chaul as its governor to build the heavily armed fort of Moro, erected on a nearby promontory to guard the mouth of the bay. But that was nearly a quarter-century after Ambar set foot in India.[15] In approximately 1571, disembarking among an array of ships converging in the harbor from places halfway around the world, Ambar now stood on the edge of the Deccan—a land not unlike Ethiopia, with its own rugged landscape, turmoil, and possibilities.

CHAPTER 3

| THE DECCAN AND MILITARY |
SLAVERY

THE DECCAN, A VAST PLATEAU covering south-central India bordered by the eastern and western Ghat mountain ranges, combines and was created out of many strands of people, cultures, and traditions.[1] Hindus, Muslims, Buddhists, Jains, and Christians were all part of the Deccan's dynamic mix during the sixteenth and seventeenth centuries. Culturally, most visible were the Marathi-speaking Hindu natives. They were followed by Muslim Indo-Turks and Persianate "Westerners" who came from the north; Arabs and their descendants, having sailed from the Middle East; Africans from the Ethiopian hinterland and Sudan taken to India as part of the military slave system; and a scattering of Europeans, namely Dutch and Portuguese merchants.[2] Deccanis were spread out among urban centers and the countryside. They were pastoralists, agriculturalists, and from freshwater fishing villages; most were landless peasants, not unlike the peasants of Malik Ambar's motherland, who also paid heavy taxes.[3]

In time, Ambar would embrace the Deccan as his own and come to know its cities and towns teeming with artisans, soldiers, street vendors, musicians, water carriers, and wandering ascetics. He would also come to know the region's countryside, especially its arid west, which received little rainfall, as the high Western Ghats—the Sahyadri mountains only thirty miles from the lush

29

seacoast—blocked much of the moisture of the southwest monsoons (the word monsoon being derived from the Arabic word *mawsim*, "season"). Separated from northern India by the Vindhya Range, a chain of mountains, hills, and forests, the Deccan had always required careful cultivation, flexibility, and foresight—characteristics Ambar would come to master in time.

The rulers of the western Deccan, the area in which Ambar became most prominent, were largely Dakhini-speaking Muslims governing predominantly Marathi-speaking Hindus. The political elite were Turko-Afghans steeped in Persian customs and traditions. Deccani courts, however, included Hindu administrators; its armies, Hindu soldiers and commanders. Cultural and social distinctions between Muslims and Hindus (which have been exaggerated in later colonial British histories as well as twentieth-century nationalist South Asian historiography) were, more than not, blurred in court life, as they were in the arts, architecture, dress, music, and religious practice of everyday life of subjects in cities and countryside.[4]

Abyssinian slave soldiers and mercenaries figured prominently in the western Deccan. By the mid-sixteenth century, Abyssinians were established across much of India as bodyguards, foot soldiers, cavalrymen, and field commanders. Indeed, for at least four generations before Ambar arrived in the Deccan, India had proven a place where Abyssinians with particular skills, talents, and ambition could rise through the ranks to positions of significant authority, some becoming nobles in their own right.

Abyssinians, or Habshis (as Africans from Ethiopia and the Sudan are called in the South Asia), were considered a trusted, outside force—that is, without kinship ties to claim Indian thrones, although in Bengal some briefly did.[5] As the Persian diplomat Nizam al-Mulk explained the thinking behind military slavery, "One obedient slave is better than three hundred sons; for the latter desire their father's death, the former long life for his master."[6]

Across the Middle East, Arabs and Persians had tapped Abyssinians as slave soldiers to fight in their armies. Likewise, and although most visible among Muslim polities, Hindu and Buddhist kingdoms and, later, Christian European powers drew upon Abyssinians in South Asia to protect or extend their interests. Ambar was therefore part of a much larger flow of Abyssinians from Africa to India. Describing this forced migration, the sixteenth-century Italian traveler Ludovico di Varthema recorded in his diary how Abyssinians were regularly taken by "Moors" (Muslims) to Zeila and from there "carried into Persia, Arabia Felix [southern Arabia] . . . and into India," covering much of the same course of Ambar's journey from Ethiopia to India.[7] However, centuries before warriors from the Horn of Africa graced the hills, valleys, palaces, and forts of the Deccan, Abyssinians landed on its western shores as merchants and sailors.

The trade that brought Ambar and so many other Abyssinians to South Asia during the sixteenth and seventeenth centuries dated to ancient times. Commercial contacts between Abyssinia and India went back nearly two thousand years: Kushana (Indian) gold coins and figurines have been excavated in Ethiopia that date from the second century B.C.E.; likewise, Abyssinians had long been making their way into India with their own products.[8] But while trade relatively peacefully flowed by sea between Ethiopia and India, battles over access to land in northwestern India's interior characterized much of that area's turbulent history. As far back as the fourth century C.E., Greeks under the command of Alexander the Great, followed by a series of successive invaders (Scythians, Huns, Turks, Mongols, and Afghans), had taken over and settled in northern India, mixing with local populations over the centuries.[9]

Islam, which Ambar had likely adopted sometime between Mocha and Baghdad, would make its first appearance in the northwestern part of India during the early eighth century when Arab forces under the Umayyads established the short-lived *al-Hind* (Sind) sultanate in the lower Indus Valley. Soon, Muslim merchants from southern Arabia were traveling to the Malabar coast of southwest India. Known as Mapilla, these Muslim merchants living under Hindu monarchs, settled, married local women, and developed their own syncretic societies, fusing southern Arabian customs with the Malayalam practices and traditions of southwest India—as with the retention of matrilineal inheritance.

While Muslims continued to trade and form communities along the western coasts of India, it was not until the early thirteenth century with the establishment of what became a series of Delhi-based Turkic dynasties (Mamluk, Khilji, Tughluq, Sayyid, and Lodi), known together as the Delhi Sultanate (1206–1526), that Islam became a lasting presence in northern India—replacing the Buddhist-led Pala Empire (eighth through twelfth centuries C.E.) in northeastern India. In contrast to the Malabar coast, Persian—not Arab—culture and conventions dominated the *darbar* (courts) of the north. Indeed, over the next five centuries, including through Ambar's era, the language of the Muslim elite in northern India was Persian. However, beginning in the fourteenth century a new language took root, Urdu, largely combining Persian with Sanskrit-based languages, specifically the Hindustani dialect Khariboli, spoken just outside of Delhi, with a scattering of Arabic words.

Urdu, born in and around the military garrisons of the Muslim armies of the north, would soon become famous for its use in poetry. Writing in both Persian and Urdu, the Sufi Amir Khusraw was one of the earliest poets to draw upon the flow and lyricism of the new language. Over time, Urdu became the principal language of Muslims across India, with local variants such as Dakhini (spoken in the western Deccan), the language that Ambar would most likely learn and use for much of his life.[10]

As with the evolution of language, the Deccan's government was a product of earlier, northern Indian influences in combination with local practices and traditions. Most influential on the Deccan's form and style of government was the Delhi Sultanate, which provided the model of governance and religious pluralism that Muslim-led polities across India followed throughout most of the early modern period. From the sixteenth through seventeenth centuries, both Mughal rule in northern India and Bahmani, followed by five-sultanate-rule in the Deccan, followed the Delhi model of generally maintaining ethnically diverse courts with loyalty to the sultan, irrespective of tribal affiliation or Muslim sectarian identity (Sunni or Shi'a). In this way, India's Muslim-led powers were not exclusively "Islamic," nor did they engage in religious wars, unlike the Adal Sultanate of Ambar's Ethiopia, which carried out this "lower" form of *jihad* (as opposed to the "higher" form—"struggle," entailing personal, spiritual striving).

While Muslim rulers in India were expected to patronize Muslim institutions—namely, the *ulema* (the Muslim legal scholars) and the *sufi shaykhs* (the moral and spiritual guides of the *ummah*)—they also lent support to non-Muslim institutions. Moreover, as the historian Barbara Metcalf explains, "Muslim spiritual and philosophical life in India evolved together with the religious life of non-Muslims. Each was responding to a shared context."[11] In terms of governance, religious pluralism therefore reflected the lived interaction and manifest fusion of otherwise institutionally distinct religions; it also fostered greater political stability. That is, as a practical matter, in order for Muslims to rule over majority Hindu populations there needed to be a degree of openness and accommodation on the part of the former—for instance, treating Hindus (as well as Buddhists) with equal protections and responsibilities as *dhimmi*, "People of the Book" (Jews and Christians).

From the Delhi Sultanate came much of the Bahmani Empire in the fourteenth century, which pressed into the Deccan and out of which came the Deccani sultanates in the early sixteenth century. In 1347 c.e., Hasan Gangu, one of the generals of the Delhi Sultan Muhammad bin Tughluq, led a revolt and established his own kingdom in the southern provinces. The forces of Bahman Shah—as the general-turned-sultan came to be called—spread. Soon his armies were exerting their authority over much of the Deccan. With the Delhi sultanates still in control of the north, the land routes to Central Asia from the Deccan were blocked, prompting an increase in Indian Ocean maritime trade via the Arabian Sea, including Persian warhorses and enslaved Africans—each of which became essential in maintaining the rule of the Deccani elite.[12] By the late fifteenth century the Bahmani Empire began to split into five warring sultanates: the Imad Shahi of Berar, the Barid Shahi of Bidar, the Adil Shahi of Bijapur, the Qutub Shahi of Golconda, and the Nizam Shahi of Ahmednagar—the sultanate in whose service Ambar was mostly closely affiliated.[13]

By the late fifteenth century the Delhi Sultanate had also broken apart, first into several kingdoms, including Bengal, Gujarat, Jaunpur, and Malwa. The Mughals would not only eclipse the Delhi Sultanate but soon control all of the regional kingdoms that had broken away from it. Like the sultanates of the Deccan, the Mughals built on conventions and practices established by the Delhi Sultanate; they extended the processes of urban and rural development started by the Delhi Sultanate, continued Turko-Afghan-Persianate dynastic rule, and governed in a pluralistic form.

With its capital at Agra, located on the banks of the Yamuna River, the Mughals had become the most powerful political force in South Asian history by the time of Ambar's arrival in India. The Mughals were wealthier and with larger populations than any of their contemporary and fellow Muslim-led powers in the world—including the Songhay of West Africa, the Persian Safavids, the Ottoman Turks, and the Sultanate of Aceh in Sumatra.

The birth of the Mughals, like those of all imperial powers, has been retold as one of right over wrong—and over tremendous odds. In brief, in 1526, the Delhi Sultanate's last ruler, Bahlul Khan Lodi, fell to the forces of Zahir-ud-din Muhammad Babur at the Battle of Panipat, just northwest of Delhi. Armed with matchlock muskets (the latest Ottoman weaponry), cavalry, and foot soldiers, Babur—who was descended from the Central Asian conqueror Timur on his father's side and from the Mongol Emperor Chingiz Khan on his mother's—marched on Delhi

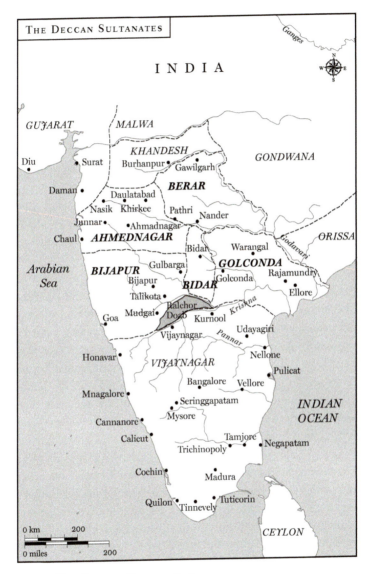

MAP 3. THE DECCAN SULTANATES

with a force of 12,000.[14] His army swelled as it approached the capital, doubling with recruits from the countryside who joined the quest to topple Lodi—a detested figure among the population according to the Mughals. Although facing a force quadruple its own size—an army of 100,000, including one hundred war elephants—Babur outmaneuvered Lodi, who was killed in the battle.

Babur's rule in northern India, however, was relatively brief—approximately four years. Accomplishing little more than establishing garrisons to mark the area under his control, Babur nevertheless created the basis for later, expansive Mughal rule. But if Babur's rule was brief, his grandson, Akbar, would compensate by ruling for nearly half a century, expanding the empire to the largest area ever ruled by a single power in India.

Akbar pushed Mughal frontiers north to Kashmir, east to Bengal, and southwest to Gujarat, just north of the Deccan. Embracing the Delhi Sultanate's policy of inclusive rule, he incorporated powerful indigenous lineages, notably Rajputs of northwestern India, who controlled their own domains. Akbar also began the dynastic custom of marrying Rajput women, most famously "Jodha Bai" (as she is popularly known), the mother of Jahangir (the next emperor and Ambar's future nemesis), who were not expected to convert to Islam. Mughal ruling elites therefore came to include not only Persians but also Central Asians, Rajputs, Arabs, and Brahmans (upper-caste Hindus). Akbar was famously open to a range of views at his court, where he welcomed into discussion Hindus, Jains, Zoroastrians, Jesuits (Catholics), and both Sunni and Shi'a Muslims. He himself eventually practiced a syncretic form of Islam that infused Sufi mysticism with other religious and philosophical outlooks and practices, including aspects of Hinduism and Zoroastrianism.

While the Mughals steadily advanced their agricultural frontier, developed their urban centers, built their armies, and increased their commercial and communication networks, the Deccan was divided, less integrated, and underorganized, making it politically unstable. On the frontiers of the mighty empire, the sultanates of the Deccan were vulnerable to conquest. Only by joining forces could they resist the Mughals, prepared to pounce on the Deccan if given the right opportunity. Geography, however, was on the Deccanis' side. The western part of the Deccan was virtually foreign to the Mughals, whose large armies were unaccustomed to its jagged terrain and narrow passages— features Ambar would later use to great effect against the imperial armies.

Although the five Deccani sultanates had remained independent of the Mughals over the course of the sixteenth century and were no longer threatened by the great Hindu-led southern Vijayanagara Empire—which was defeated through a combined effort of Deccani forces at the Battle of Talikota in 1565—the threat of a northern invasion loomed heavily over the rulers of the plateau, especially those on the front lines. Located in the northwestern part of the Deccan, the Sultanate of Ahmednagar was the first of the kingdoms that would need to be conquered by the Mughals if they were going to conquer the region as a whole.[15]

Just as war consumed the Ethiopia of Ambar's youth, so too would it consume the Deccan of his adulthood. Here in western India, where Abyssinian slave-soldiers—military slaves—were in large and steady demand, Ambar would once again change masters. This time, though, he was mentored by a far more powerful person. In approximately 1571 he entered the Indian side of the military slave system in Ahmednagar. As the comparative literary scholar Thomas Christensen notes, "The idea behind the institution of the military slave was that by removing warriors from their family ties, factionalism based on kinship could be held in check. The same idea was behind the janissary troops of the Ottomans, who were mainly preadolescent Christians from the Balkans, given up to the empire as a kind of tax called *devshirme*; they were given military and Islamic training, and were supposed to remain celibate."[16] Although unclear to him at the time of his capture in Ethiopia, and perhaps even during his years in Baghdad, Ambar was actually part of the much larger military slave system of the Indian Ocean world.

Soon after arriving in India, Mir Qasim sold Ambar to Mirak Dabir—better known as Chengiz Khan, none other than the chief minister (*peshwa*) of the Sultanate of Ahmednagar. Khan, a Habshi who was once a slave himself, had risen to his position in the court and now had one thousand military slaves of his own under his command. Khan was among a number of high-ranking court officials in the Deccan who had been procuring African slaves in a systematic manner for their armies during the sixteenth century—just as Bahmani officials had done in the century prior. Because of their access to the seaports of western India, and therefore maritime trade from East Africa and the Middle East, the sultanates of Ahmednagar and Bijapur probably had the highest number of Abyssinians among the five Deccani sultanates.[17] The fact is suggested in the numerous paintings from the period depicting African soldiers and nobles.[18]

Ambar joined Khan's many slave-soldiers, among whom he quickly distinguished himself. His stature and presence made him an impressive figure. Described by the Dutch merchant Pieter van den Broecke as "tall and strong," Ambar came to Khan's attention. The *peshwa* took it upon himself to mentor the Arabic-speaking Abyssinian whose disposition and background apparently made him stand out as suitable for leadership training (it is also conceivable that they shared a common Oromo background).[19] Ambar would therefore enter a new phase of service and a new kind of training.

In practice, once deracinated—that is, taken far from their family and home—military slaves' relationships with their masters, especially in the Deccan, were largely based on mutual benefit. On the one hand, the slave being disconnected from immediate family and tribe needed a connection (that is, someone with standing and resources); on the other hand, masters (be they field commanders, royal administrators, or monarchs) needed the protection of their slaves. For monarchs, African slaves were especially important since they could not claim lineage in the South Asian sociopolitical context. In time, the slave–master relationship became one of client–patron, as it was common practice for military slaves to be considered free once their master died and then seek patrons to support their work. The social and political need created an ever-growing number of Africans in India, who often scaled the hierarchy of authority over the course of their lifetimes, marrying into local populations and even becoming slaveholders themselves. Upward mobility was not uncommon among military slaves—perhaps even to be expected among the most talented. This kind of slavery in the Deccan was, therefore, in marked contrast to other forms of slavery, especially those practiced in the Americas, where slavery was lifelong and remained a system based principally on force or the threat of force.

The historian Richard M. Eaton notes the significantly different form of enslavement that military slavery entailed in the Middle East and South Asia from other forms of slavery in the Indian Ocean world. As Eaton writes, "Living in the same surroundings and eating the same food as their masters, such slaves not only became fictive kin of their masters, but they did so . . . even *before* becoming manumitted." In this way, the institution of military slavery in the Indian Ocean world tended to be a self-terminating process, rather than a condition that was lifelong. In Ahmednagar, Eaton notes, "men who had begun their careers as culturally alien slaves without kin, over time became integrated into their host society, acquired kin, and embraced a Deccani regional identity." This process helps to explain why there is hardly a mention of Habshi slaves in Nizam Shahi service ever being formally manumitted. Pointing to seventeenth-century foreign travelers in India, Eaton describes how such African slaves were indeed "tied to their Deccani masters by close and affectionate bonds," an assertion that suggests a very different kind of slavery than what largely emerges in the Atlantic world.[20]

Ambar would serve Khan as a personal aide in managing the Nizam Shahi domains; under his guidance he had an opportunity to begin to study in real time the ways of the court, the art of war, and the workings of the civil and military administration of the state. Not surprisingly, Ambar rose quickly at the court under Khan's guidance, but all this abruptly changed. Although Khan would never see Ambar's star rise to its highest point, those who followed him did. In time, Khan's protégé became known to ministers, merchants, princes, peasants, soldiers, slaves, sultans, and even emperors from South Asia to Western Europe (ironically, Ambar was and remains little known in East Africa). At Ambar's height of power, the Nizam Shahi of the western Deccan was simply referred to as "Ambar's land."

Although Ambar became *de facto* ruler of the Sultanate of Ahmednagar, he never claimed the kingdom as his own. Instead, he invoked the concept of *namak halal*, or "fidelity to salt"—serving faithfully on behalf of the Nizam Shah, whoever that person might be. As Eaton describes, "'Eating the salt' or 'fidelity to salt' refers to the oath that binds a patron and client through mutual obligations of protection and loyalty."[21] The idea was deep-seated in the political culture of India, dating to the Delhi Sultanate and continuing with the Mughals—although variously practiced (like any ideology).[22] Ambar astutely drew upon this concept and tradition to advance his interests.

For two Mughal emperors, Akbar and his son Jahangir, Ambar proved to be more than just a menace on *their* frontier but an unconquerable foe, a frustrating rebel whose cunning defiance was intolerable, even maddening. For the people of the western Deccan, however, Ambar meant something different: In fits and starts, and then steadily over time, the Abyssinian slave-soldier-turned-regent emerged as their true leader, if not true king.

CHAPTER 4

AHMEDNAGAR AND
NAMAK HALAL

THE RISE OF HIS MASTER CHENGIZ KHAN from military slave to chief minister left a deep impression on Malik Ambar. In Khan's example lay the possibility for Ambar's precipitous advancement, but Khan was not his sole influence. The impact of lesser-known people on Ambar's life, his actions, and his ways of thinking— others with whom he walked, others with whom he shared his meals, laughed and talked; those who cooked for him, washed his clothes, cut his hair, and sold him goods—remain less known. We get an idea of Ambar's flexible demeanor when, many years later, the Dutchman Pieter van den Broecke notes his sense of humor during an extended meeting where he was presented with gifts and had a chance to observe the Regent Minister interacting with others who had also come to meet him, seek his counsel, and receive his permission for passage through the realm. But few such personal accounts exist. Mostly, we hear of Ambar's battle-field accomplishments, which, although certainly an important part of who he was, represented only one of his dimensions.

Ambar did not live, work, or fight in isolation; he was not a singular phenomenon whose individual abilities of the mind and discipline of the heart propelled him to stardom. Like any other person, he was the cumulative product of those with whom he interacted and those he observed. From what is known, he must have been a particularly keen observer, noting others' strengths and weaknesses, learning from them, and assessing a range of situations in order to determine his next moves. Occupying Ambar's circles were prominent figures whose lessons, successes, and failures he could, and did, learn from.

Few figures in the history of the Deccan stir the kind of passion and admiration as the person in whose footsteps Ambar would also follow: Chand Bibi. A woman of exceptional refinement, intellect, and determination, she was the daughter of Hussein Nizam Shah I of Ahmednagar, sister of his successor, and widow of Ali Adil Shah of Bijapur. She served as Bijapur's Regent from 1580 to 1590 before assuming the Regency of Ahmednagar five years later. Appearing in several paintings hawking on horseback, Bibi played sitar, painted as a hobby, spoke at least five languages (including Persian, Dakhini, and Marathi), and in 1595 led the Deccan's military defense against the Mughals.

Like Ambar, whose calculated and determined rebelliousness Bibi helped to ignite, she led as Regent of Ahmednagar with a kind of fierce loyalty, embodying Deccani independence and serving as an exemplar of resistance to northern imperial aggression. While never assuming the formal role of Sultana (although others called her by this title), she practiced the notion of *namak halal* (fidelity to salt). In years to come, Ambar would draw upon this ideology to maintain his *de facto* rule in the Deccan: He served the Nizam Shah, even if the sultan was only a figurehead.

If Khan's mentoring opened up the gates to Ambar for learning the ways of the court and state operations, Bibi's example taught him how to fight against insuperable odds. But it was Ambar's adroitness, his decisive yet flexible leadership—from handling palace intrigue to negotiating the wider politics of the Deccan—that allowed him to do what neither Khan nor Bibi was ultimately able to do: survive.

Sadly, in 1574, Khan was murdered—the result of jealous court officials who led the Nizam Shah to believe that the *peshwa* was working against him.[1] The untimely death of the Habshi statesman was certainly a blow to the sultanate of Ahmednagar, already wracked with internal problems and soon consumed by conflict over royal ascendency. Ambar, meanwhile, who had become close to Khan, was undoubtedly shaken by the sudden turn of events—and was likely both deeply angered and saddened by the travesty. (Ambar would later name his second son after him.)

Following the death of Ambar's mentor and master, Khan's widow freed him, adding formality to the common practice in military slavery in India of *de facto* freedom upon one's master's death. As Eaton notes, "[The informal process of manumission] seems to have been so common as not even to have warranted notice in contemporary Persian chronicles."[2] With little to offer Ambar materially—as the murdered minister's property was taken away by the royal court—the deliberate act of manumission by Khan's wife was perhaps a gesture of gratitude for his loyalty and service to her murdered husband.

After Khan's death Ambar had little choice but to join the Nizam Shahi army at a minor rank, working as a mercenary soldier. It was a time in which the sultanate was marred by a host of internal problems, heightened rivalries, and factionalism. As the historian Radhey Shyam notes, Ambar experienced from "close quarter the consequences of civil war and party strife and did not fail to understand that the worst days for the kingdom lay ahead."[3] According to this interpretation, Ambar witnessed a period of moral and political decline in the kingdom. Working for one commander after another, he remained in the Nizam Shahi army until he decided it was time to leave, going briefly to Golconda and then to Bijapur, where he remained for over the next decade and a half, working his way up to midlevel command. It was during this time that Ambar married Bibi Karima, a Siddi woman—"took" or "got" a wife is how it is described in historical records, as she may have been purchased.[4] Whatever the particular circumstances of their initial encounter, the couple lived a

Chand Bibi hawking on horse, 18th c. Deccan School, gouache heightened with gold on paper.

long life together and had four children: two sons, Fateh Khan and Chengiz Khan, and two daughters, Shahir Bano and Azija Bano (Fateh, the elder son, and their daughter would both later figure in the politics of the Deccan).[5]

Ambar would have begun serving in Bijapur's military at the tail-end of the reign of Ali Adil Shah I, Bibi's husband—that is, before the sultan was killed in 1579 and the boy-sultan, Ibrahim Adil Shah II, assumed the throne under Bibi's ten-year Regency starting in 1580. Ambar likely developed friendships and cama-raderie in the southern sultanate during his late twenties and thirties while also raising his own family. Being on the western coast of India, Ahmednagar and Bijapur received the largest number of African military slaves, many of whom became mer-cenaries, some rising to positions as nobles—African nobles in the Deccan. Ambar therefore had other Habshi role models to draw upon.

Among those whom he could have also looked up to—albeit at a distance—was the female Regent of Bijapur, Chand Bibi, under whom he served for a decade, even though it was multiple levels down in the hierarchy of command. Ambar was likely im-pressed by and perhaps even admired Bibi as a female leader among the many men in the court. One can imagine Ambar with other Habshi commanders standing in formation as she reviewed the sultan's troops, or perhaps being part of a *darbar*, where he witnessed the way in which she handled a variety of state affairs, including foreign dignitaries and the requests of subjects of the Adil Shah.[6]

In about 1590, as Bibi was stepping down from her position as Regent, an "Abyssinian party" began to take control of Bijapur, but its members were still "willing to give up their power to whomever [Bibi] chose," expressing their deference and respect for the Sultana.[7] Ambar, who remained at midlevel command, may have been a minor partner of this "Abyssinian party"; it was either Bibi's husband, Ali, or Ibrahim Adil Shah II, the Sultan of Bijapur—who had finally come of age—who gave Ambar the title "Malik."[8]

Despite the new title of distinction, the Adil Shahi of Bijapur was limiting to Ambar, who probably felt as though he was not advancing fast enough in terms of level of command or compensation. Although free, Ambar was without a strong and influential patron who could further advance him. War, however, would provide new opportunities for Ambar, as the Mughals, once again, cast their eyes upon the Deccan.

Nearly two decades earlier, in 1573, and less than a year before Khan was murdered, Emperor Akbar had set his sights on the Deccan. In that year, having conquered most of northern India, the emperor received a report from one of his special envoys that Ahmednagar was in political turmoil. Mughal conquest of the Deccan depended on capturing Ahmednagar because of its critical geographic location in the northwest corner of the plateau. In the year following Khan's death, divisions split the court over royal succession; conditions were ripe for a Mughal attack, as the Nizam Shahi was in disarray. However, with a rebellion erupting in the eastern provinces of northern India, Akbar was pressed to turn his attention away from the Deccan—a decision he came to regret, as years passed before another opportunity of the kind presented itself again.

Finally, in April 1595, Akbar took Deccani matters into his own hands, at first using diplomacy. He decided to make overtures to the sultanates, with the ultimate aim of bringing them under his suzerainty with the threat of force implicit in his demands. The response was perhaps to be expected: Bijapur and Golconda deflected with "costly gifts and polite words."[9] However, in Ahmednagar, Bibi's elder brother, Burhan Nizam Shah II, openly opposed Akbar by refusing to give audience to his ambassadors. Furious by the disrespect accorded to his delegation, Akbar directed his son Prince Daniyal to remind Burhan of his proper place on the Empire's frontier. But before this could happen the sultan passed away. Burhan's son, Ibrahim, assumed the throne; but as quickly as he became Nizam Shah, he was killed in battle during a sudden outbreak of war with Bijapur. Confusion now reigned as several Deccani figures promoted their own candidates to serve as Sultan of Ahmednagar. This time, Akbar would not wait to strike.

Ikhlas Khan with a page and a petition by the artist Muhammad Khan, Bijapur, mid-17th c., opaque watercolor and gold on paper.

The power vacuum in Ahmednagar that followed the death of Ibrahim Nizam Shah prompted Bibi to go to Ahmednagar to press the royal claim of Bahadur—the next son of her late brother Burhan Nizam Shah II—to the throne. Ahmednagar's *peshwa* Miyan Manjhu Dakhni, however, quickly put up a young boy named Ahmad as a way of protecting his own position in the court. But when it was discovered that Ahmad was not related to the royal family, the Abyssinian nobleman Ikhlas Khan promoted yet another child, Moti Shah, for the throne. Finally, adding to this claim was the Bijapuri Habshi commander Abhang

Khan's candidate, Miran Shah Ali, the son of the late Burhan Nizam Shah I, who was living under the protection of Ibrahim Adil Shah II of Bijapur.[10]

Caught in the whirlwind of competing figures and forces vying for position and power in Ahmednagar, Manjhu panicked. Doing the unthinkable, he invited the "lion and the sun"—the *sher-u-khurshid*—into the Deccan in order to intervene in the situation (the lion and sun were the symbols of the Mughal's *a'alam*, or flag, emblazoned in gold on a dark green background). The Emperor immediately instructed another of his sons, Prince Murad, to lead Imperial troops into the Deccan. By the time Manjhu realized what a colossal mistake he had made by inviting the Mughals into the Deccan, it was too late. Facing the option of either standing his ground and fighting or fleeing, he chose to flee. An Abyssinian nobleman named Shamshir Khan Habshi stated what others surely thought: "To fly from the enemy's army without contemplating battle and using the sword and spear, and leaving the plains of the dominion and all the subjects to be trampled upon by the enemy's army, does not commend itself to men of sincerity and faith."[11]

Manjhu countered: "The enemy's force is double that of the Dakhan . . . It is absurd for a few drops of rain to claim an equality with the infinite ocean, or for the insignificant motes to imagine themselves equal to the sun-beams."[12] His justification was one of tactical retreat and entailed seeking the help of Bijapur to the south and Golconda to the east to fight the Mughals in a united front, but also allowing Ahmednagar to fall. Defiant, Bibi took the lead in defending the Fort of Ahmednagar, the seat of the Sultanate, in the process proclaiming the young Bahadur as Nizam Shah.

Earlier in 1595, frustrated with the level of support and responsibility he was being given in Bijapur, Ambar left the Adil Shahi with a corps of 150 loyal cavalrymen and returned to Ahmednagar, where he entered the service of the Habshi commander Abhang Khan, who was pressing for his candidate for the Nizam Shahi throne. The timing brought Ambar directly into the

Interior of the Fort of Ahmednagar, pen-and-ink drawing by William Miller, 1831.

theater of conflict and soon war, as the Mughals descended into the Deccan with their heavy cannon, cavalry units, archers, and legions of foot soldiers, armed with swords and spears.

Rallying the Nizam Shahi troops that now came under her command, Bibi was also able to convince Abhang Khan to stand with her while winning over a number of other Abyssinian nobles, including Ikhlas Khan. Meanwhile, she asked her nephew Ibrahim Adil Shah II, who had sent reinforcements to Bibi, to contain Manjhu, who had taken refuge in Bijapur. Inspiring her would-be partners to take a stance together, she secured a coalition of Abyssinians—"African *amirs*"—and Indo-Turk Deccanis to keep the Mughals from overtaking Ahmednagar.[13]

The Mughals were now encamped at the perimeter of the Fort of Ahmednagar, to which they began to lay siege with their powerful artillery. Ambar, now in Bibi's coalition by way of Abhang Khan, set out to break the Mughal supply lines feeding the siege. On the night of December 21, 1595, Ambar led a surprise attack on the Mughals and broke through. Cutting their principal line of communication, Ambar's cavalry disrupted the northern imperialists' source of supply and seized provisions; however, they were unable to do much more damage. Overwhelmed by the Mughal force, Ambar and his soldiers dispersed into the night.[14]

Bibi and her troops held steady as the siege dragged on, punctuated by deafening blows of Mughal cannonballs pounding the fort's walls. But then the Mughals received a break. Concentrating their attack on one part of the fort, the imperialists breached the citadel. The Persian historian, and contemporary of Ambar, Muhammed Qasim Ferishta describes what happened next: "Immediately as the breach was made, many of the principal officers of the besieged prepared for flight. Chand Bibi, on the contrary, put on armour, and with a veil on her face, and naked sword in her hand, flew to defend the breach. This instance of intrepidity brought back the fugitives who now one and all joined her."[15] Bibi's bravery and show of force kept her men from scattering, closed the breach, and prevented the Nizam Shahi from being overtaken then and there.

Prince Murad launched a final attack on the fort, but the Deccanis once again held firm and repelled the imperialists. The Mughals, whose supplies were now running low and whose troops were visibly exhausted after four months of siege warfare, became resigned to their weakened position outside of the fort. Ambar, meanwhile, continued to harass the Mughals with hit-and-run night operations from the countryside that further demoralized soldiers and generals alike. Mostly, though, with the sound of cannon fire, the faint smell of gunpowder, and billowing smoke in the distance, he observed the tenacity of the Deccani forces persevering inside of the fort under Bibi's leadership.

Having reached a stalemate, on March 14, 1596, Ahmednagar and the Mughals began negotiating a peace settlement. Tensions quickly arose as the talks began around issues of gender, race, and ethnicity—issues of power that Ambar would clearly wrestle with in coming years. During the peace talks what also becomes apparent is that the notion of *namak halal* served as an effective way of unifying dissimilar groups of people. The concept and practice of this "fidelity to salt" had also made it possible for Bibi to maintain her diverse coalition of Persians (or "Westerners," as they were called), Indo-Turks, and Abyssinians—a strategy Ambar would use to great effect in binding Ahmednagar's disparate constituencies.

Meeting outside the fort's thick but shaken walls, and with Deccani flags unfurled, the elder statesman and ambassador of the Ahmednagar sultanate Afzal Khan approached Prince Murad, who was flanked by his commanding officers. Khan opened the peace talks by boldly challenging Mughal claims to Deccani soil, to which one of the Mughal generals at the side of the Prince exclaimed: "What nonsense is this? You, like a eunuch, are keeping a woman [Chand Bibi] in the fort in the hope that she will come to your aid … [Prince Murad] is the son of his Majesty [the Emperor], at whose court many kings do service. Do you imagine that the crows and kites of the Deccan, who squat like ants or locusts over a few spiders, can cope with the descendant of Timur and his famous *amirs* . . . each of whom has conquered countries ten times as large as the Deccan? . . . You, who are men of the same race [Persian] as ourselves, should not throw yourselves away."[16]

As Eaton carefully notes, the Mughal general was at once challenging the ambassador's masculinity while pitting him against those of non-Persian descent (the "crows and kites," being a reference to the Abyssinians and Indo-Turkic Deccanis whom Khan was representing).

The ambassador solemnly replied: "For forty years I have eaten the salt of the sultans of the Deccan . . . There is no better way to die than to be slain for one's benefactor . . . Moreover, it should be evident to you that the people of this country are hostile towards [you]. I myself am a Westerner [Persian] and a well-wisher of the emperor, and I consider it to be in his interest to withdraw the Prince's great *amirs* from the area of this fort."[17]

Despite the tense opening to the peace talks, a settlement was eventually reached. The accord gave the Deccanis more land while acknowledging nominal Mughal suzerainty, *but there would be no occupation of the Deccan.* The imperialists decamped and began their slow march back to the northern frontier—a great river of soldiers reversing course, with bullocks in tow pulling the Mughals' heavy siege guns gone silent.

The peace brought about through Bibi's vigorous defense of the Fort of Ahmednagar, in which Ambar had played a secondary role, bought the Deccanis time. The Mughals, meanwhile, were left wanting and began to employ new measures to try to destabilize the Deccanis. Over the next years Bibi served as Regent of Ahmednagar—*de facto* ruler—with her brother's son on the Nizam Shahi throne. But the peace did not last. Jealousies and rivalries arose at the court of Ahmednagar, prompted by generous salaries and lucrative posts offered by the Mughals to peel away Deccani court officials and field commanders. Bibi began losing confidence in those around her, who were now vacillating under renewed Mughal pressure; the coalition she had brought together in 1595 was coming apart.

With dark clouds gathering overhead, Bibi sent an urgent message through a trusted African eunuch to have the sultan taken to the Fort of Junnar, located just northwest of Ahmednagar. A rumor, however, spread quickly that instead of trying to protect the Nizam Shah, Bibi had given herself over to the Mughals and was preparing to surrender both the fort and the sultanate she had so valiantly defended several years earlier. In the melee that followed Bibi was killed by some of her own troops. Proud, if not paranoid, they were convinced that she was committing treachery.

Without Bibi at the helm to keep Ahmednagar's soldiers in line and the nobles in check, on August 16, 1600, the Mughals broke through the Fort of Ahmednagar, arrested Sultan Bahadur Nizam Shah, and took him prisoner deep into Mughal territory. Carrying him to the Fort of Gwalior in northern India, the sultan was swept far into the northern hinterland, some six hundred miles away from Ahmednagar (three times the distance Ambar walked from Hararghe to Zeila). The chances of the young Nizam Shah ever being returned home were as remote as where he was taken; for all intents and purposes, he was politically dead. But in the fallout over the Mughal occupation of the Ahmednagar, Ambar re-emerged from the countryside. This time, however— and in full stride—he would pick up Bibi's torch and reignite the anti-imperial struggle. And he was not alone.

CHAPTER 5

| REBELS, REGENCY, AND RACE |

FOR THE MUGHALS, THE CAPTURE of the Fort of Ahmednagar in 1600 was the first step in the conquest of the Deccan. As Emperor Akbar's court chronicler Abu'l-Fazl writes in the *Akbarnama*, after storming the Deccani citadel and putting "1,500 of the garrison . . . to the sword," the Mughals took hold of "[v]aluable jewels, embroidered articles, a noble library . . . and twenty-five elephants"—that is, among "many other things."[1] Tragic as this was for the Nizam Shahi, the fall of the sultanate presented a new opportunity for Malik Ambar, whose ambitions soared.

In the nearly five years between Chand Bibi's defense of the Fort of Ahmednagar in 1595 and the Mughal capture and imprisonment of Bahadur Nizam Shah, Ambar increased his following across the western Deccan. Not only did he inherit the army of his former Bijapuri commander Abhang Khan, who was captured by rival troops, but owing to his success in harassing Mughal forces, raiding their supply convoys, and even making forays into lands just north of the Deccani border, Ambar drew hundreds of combatants into his ranks. By the end of 1596 he had over three thousand cavalrymen under his command; many of the Deccani troops that had disbanded into the countryside after the siege of Ahmednagar joined him, as would local bandits and others he brought under his control.[2] Battlefield success, raids, and, most importantly, booty, as it were, generated fame and following;

former royal soldiers and outlaws—rebels one and all—were now part of Ambar's growing multiethnic, multiracial army.

Ambar also drew the attention of others, some from very far afield—indeed overseas. Given the strategic location of his area of influence in the Deccan, especially in the northwestern part of the region—that is, the area just below the Mughal's southern frontier and along India's western coast with access to key ports south of Surat—Ambar's reputation caught the attention of the Spanish king halfway around the world with economic interests in the region.

Correspondence between Spain's King Philip II, who also ruled Portugal, and his viceroys in India (Goa had been under Portuguese control since 1510) suggest the geographic extent of Ambar's authority in the western Deccan starting in the late 1590s. Just as Ambar's contemporary the pirate Francis Drake had been made legitimate (even knighted) by the Queen of England, Elizabeth I—as Drake's pirating of Spanish vessels was beneficial to the English crown—so too, it seems, Ambar could be spoken of in favorable terms by an imperial power if needed as an ally. So while King Philip II offered up to twenty thousand ducats for the capture of Drake, described as a blight on Spanish treasure ships in the Pacific, the Iberians looked to Ambar as a possible ally in serving as a buffer against expanding Mughal imperialism in the Indian Ocean. In a series of letters to viceroys Dom Francisco de Gama and Ayres de Saldana, King Philip II refers to the "kingdom of Mellique" and describes him as a "chief" of Chaul and Dhabul. Despite such recognition, Ambar remained an illegitimate figure in the Mughal frontier, a rebel without proper title or position.

Through ongoing recruitment and training, by 1600, Ambar's forces grew to seven thousand cavalry, comprising Abyssinians, Muslim Deccanis, and Hindu Marathas—a multiracial, multiethnic force that broadly shared a regional identity distinct from the northern Mughals.[3] With the Nizam Shah locked away and the kingdom in disarray, Ambar decided on a bold new strategy:

Instead of merely harassing the Mughals, picking off their supplies, and playing the role of a minor chief, he decided to revive the Nizam Shahi sultanate and rally the kingdom in anti-Mughal struggle around the notion of fidelity to a new Nizam Shah. He began by looking for a suitable member of the royal family whom he could install and for whom he could then serve as Regent.

As part of Ambar's strategy to establish his Regency he created a marriage alliance. As Eaton notes, "Finding a twenty-year-old scion of Ahmednagar's royal family in neighboring Bijapur, he promoted the cause of this youth as future ruler of a reconstituted Nizam Shahi state ... [and in order to] bind his royal candidate more closely to him, Ambar offered him his own daughter in marriage." In 1600, the young couple were married at Ambar's headquarters at Parenda, a fort located seventy-five miles southeast of now Mughal-occupied Ahmednagar. Following what would have been an elaborate wedding ceremony, Ambar presided over the installation of his new son-in-law as Sultan Murtaza Nizam Shah II—the son of Miran Shah 'Ali, the brother of the last sultan of Ahmednagar. As expected, the sultan appointed Ambar Regent Minister, acknowledging the Abyssinian's *de facto* rule over the kingdom.[4]

Although Ambar was now Regent of the Nizam Shahi, the sultanate remained divided over who would lead the anti-imperial cause. Soon competing for this role was a veteran military leader named Raju Dakhni. Once the personal attendant of the Deccani commander Sa'adat Khan, who had since defected to the Mughals' side, Raju proved a formidable rival to Ambar while claiming allegiance to the very same Nizam Shah. Abhang Khan had played a key role in keeping Raju on the side of the Nizam Shahi when Sa'adat was bribed into the Mughal services during the siege of Ahmednagar. Imploring Raju to stay and fight for the sultanate, Khan said to him, "Fortune has made you a great man ... Sa'adat [Khan] has turned traitor to Nizam Shah and gone over to the Mughals ... act bravely, because the reward of fidelity to salt is greatness. Guard carefully the territory and forts now in your hands, and try to increase them."[5]

Mughal armies as depicted in the Akbarnama, *opaque watercolor, ink and gold on paper, India, circa 1596–1600.*

Over the next few years, Ambar and Raju both waged war against the Mughals in the area south of the Vindhya Range, a rocky and rugged land, with Raju in the northwestern part of Ahmednagar and Ambar in the remainder of the Deccani Sultanate—both armies infused with Chand Bibi's defiant spirit against northern imperialism, long forming part of the region's political fabric.[6] Like their forerunners, the Bahmanis, the Deccanis were animated by a fierce sense of independence, so much so that at times the various autonomous sultanates left themselves vulnerable to northern imperial attack because of their infighting. Whoever did emerge as leader of the anti-Mughal forces would need to keep down the "turbulent spirits" of the Deccan—or, perhaps more accurately, figure out ways of turning those "spirits" against the north.

While the rank and file of the Deccani forces under Ambar and Raju's separate commands (which sometimes included the armies of Golconda and Bijapur) were anti-Mughal, soldiers were as much driven by material interests, which may explain Ambar's success in gathering soldiers as military victories and plundering resulted in the spoils of war. Some soldiers were apparently also driven by their own fidelity toward Ambar. Known as a daring and smart commander, Ambar personally led his troops in guerrilla operations and spent time with them in the camps. Commanding his troops meant commanding their respect, so much so that many gave their own lives to save his. On several occasions, including at Nandere in 1601 and Qandahar in 1602, he narrowly escaped being captured or being killed because of his brave and loyal soldiers. Ferishta writes that at Nandare, "where a severe action took place, in which many soldiers were slain on both sides . . . Mullik Ambur, who lay wounded on the field, was only saved by the devoted gallantry of his attendants from falling a prisoner into the enemy's hands." Ferishta goes on to note that Ambar's soldiers were only able to save him "after losing a number of men."[7]

Battling the Mughals was not Ambar's only immediate preoccupation; war in the Deccan was matched by intrigues in his court. In 1602, just as the esteemed Mughal court chronicler Abu'l-Fazl was murdered by Prince Salim (soon Emperor Jahangir) because of his opposition to the prince's accession to the throne, so too was Ambar's rule filled with those who would and did betray him. Meanwhile, the Portuguese were growing nervous about the possibility of Ambar attacking Goa, yet another site of brewing conflict.[8]

Then, on October 27, 1605, after weeks of suffering from an attack of dysentery, Emperor Akbar passed away. Although by 1601 he had annexed Gujarat, Khandesh, and Berar, and much of the Godavari Basin, he also withstood a rebellion by his own son, Prince Salim, and was further disheartened by the bickering between Salim and his grandson Prince Khusrau. After nearly fifty years' reign and having expanded the empire to its fullest yet, he died dispirited by family feud and unable to wrest control of the Deccan. Nevertheless, his accomplishments were unprecedented. The *Akbarnama* expresses in verse the passing of the great Mughal emperor:[9]

> In the garden the glory of the jasmine faded
> As when the face of the moon is eclipsed,
> The market of flowers and spring broke up,
> The world's grandeur was dissolved . . .[10]

Akbar's son, Prince Salim, assumed the imperial Mughal throne as Nur-ud-Din Muhammed Jahangir. Despite differences with his father, the prince, now emperor, was just as fervent, if not more so, about Mughal expansion into the Deccan—and more vulnerable to enemies in and out his court, despite the efforts of his politically astute and influential wives Ruqaiya and Salima, and his grandmother (Akbar's mother), Maryam Makani. As the writer Indu Sundaresan imagines, "With the empire as vast as it was, a change of the crown from one head to another seemed to provoke every enemy king into action. They sent messages of congratulations, of course, writing with one hand while the other rested on a sword."[11] Not only would Emperor Jahangir face internal dissent and the machinations of rival, albeit vassal kings, like his own father he also had to contend with outright rebellion. Within a year of becoming emperor, Jahangir's son Prince Khusrau led a rebellion to overthrow him. Caught in 1606, Prince Khusrau was dragged before his father, the emperor, who summarily blinded him and put two thousand of his followers to death.

Although pressures on Ambar were on a smaller scale than those faced by the emperor in the north, they were no less meaningful. At the beginning of 1603, three of Ambar's own officers, Venkat Rao, Farhad Khan, and Malik Sandal, rebelled against him. Given tacit support by the Adil Shah of Bijapur, Rao, Khan, and Sandal were eventually overwhelmed by Ambar, who imprisoned the first and had the others "take to their heels" and make terms with him. Although Ambar himself had temporarily entered into a treaty with the Mughals in order to stall for time while dealing with his own rebels, he made it clear that "he was a true and loyal servant of the Nizam Shah's family and was ready to support it with his last breath."[12] Throughout this period, Ambar's chief rival in the Deccan remained Raju, despite both pledging loyalty to the same king.

While Ambar and Raju were relatively evenly matched in the field, larger conditions favored the Abyssinian in the balance of power. The Mughal chronicler Nawab Shahnawaz Khan writes in his *Maasir Al-Umara*, "in Upper India the contentions of [Jahangir], the death of Akbar, and the rebellion of [Prince] Khusrau quickly followed one another. Malik 'Ambar was able at his ease to increase his power, and he collected numerous soldiers, and took possession of most of the Imperial estates." The state of flux and transition in northern India in 1605–1606 therefore allowed Ambar to regain lost lands and expand his power in the region. But, as Shahnawaz Khan continues, "When the power of Jahangir was consolidated, armies were repeatedly appointed. Malik Ambar was sometimes defeated, and sometimes victorious, but did not cease to oppose."[13]

*Emperor Jahangir shooting arrow at Malik Ambar by the artist
Abu'l Hasan, circa 1616. 19th c. copy of original painting located
at the Chester Beatty Library, Dublin.*

Although the Mughals were not able to advance their control much further south into the Deccan because of Raju and Ambar's defense, they maintained a large military presence with units stationed in forward positions along the Mughal–Deccani border. During this period, part of what also made it possible for Ambar to gain ground (in addition to the turmoil faced by the Mughal rulers in the north) was the fact that Raju was on the front lines, positioned immediately south of the empire. For Ambar, Raju served the anti-imperial cause while sheltering him from the harshest northern attacks and counterattacks. Weakened, Raju ultimately paid the price. Ambar took full advantage of the Mughals being engaged with Raju during this time to take back land that had fallen under imperial control since 1600, further strengthening his own position.

In 1607 Ambar decided once and for all to end the rivalry with Raju, whose reputation by this point had become one of highhandedness among his soldiers and abuse among the population. Perhaps feeling justified, Ambar "marched at the head of ten thousand cavalry from Parenda against Junnar" and arrested Raju, who was imprisoned. Meanwhile Ambar captured both Daulatabad and Junnar, strategic locations in the war against the Mughals.[14] Imperial attacks from the north nevertheless continued; Jahangir, finally free to turn his attention to the Deccan, would direct one after another of his armies to destroy Ambar, who carefully avoided pitched battles, since his forces were invariably smaller than those of the Mughals.[15]

In the midst of war, Ambar, as *de facto* ruler of the now revived and consolidated Sultanate of Ahmednagar, was also responsible for the flow of trade and civil administration within his realm. Among the many fronts he was handling were negotiations with Europeans traders. While the Spanish–Portuguese crown looked to Ambar as an ally against the Mughals, Iberian power in the Indian Ocean was quickly diminishing with the rise of the English and Dutch trading companies—the English East India Company, founded in 1600, and the Dutch East India

Company (*Vereenigde Oostindische Compagnie*, or VOC), founded in 1602. Ambar decided to check English merchant advances starting in 1609 and would re-engage them several more times over the coming years.[16]

While Ambar battled the Mughal armies, dealt with challenging figures, and tackled foreign traders, he also sought ways of enhancing his authority, position, and security in the Deccan. A way of doing so was to have his son marry into the region's nobility. While his daughter's marriage to Murtaza Nizam Shah II in 1600 had already given Ambar official ties to Ahmednagar's nobility, he sought broader and deeper connections in the region: In 1609 Ambar's son, Fateh Khan, married the daughter of the Habshi Yaqut Khan, perhaps the most important nobleman of Bijapur at the time. The marriage, which took place in February, was a spectacular display of pomp and circumstance, commensurate with the standards of the two kingdoms' nobility. As the biographer Radhey Shyam notes, the wedding celebration in Bijapur "was performed amidst great rejoicings which continued for forty days . . . About twenty thousand *huns* (Rs. 80,000) [was spent] on the fireworks alone."[17] Ambar had become one of the most highly connected leaders in the Deccan by securing kinship ties with the Nizam Shahi dynasty through his daughter while enjoying kinship ties with the most prominent Habshi aristocratic family in Bijapur through his son.

Improving Ambar's social standing in the Deccan was one of several ways of increasing his power and authority and, as it will become clear, ensuring a degree of protection from Bijapur in the future.[18] Another way of strengthening his position was to simply sweep away nearby opposition (not unlike what he did with Raju). An incident involving his daughter in the Nizam Shah's palace in 1610 compelled him to take such swift and dramatic action.

Ahmednagar, like Bijapur, reflected the Deccan's ethnic diversity, with a large Maratha population but with a particularly visible Abyssinian presence. The African character of the western

Fateh Khan, opaque watercolor on paper, circa 1620.

Deccan—from elite gatherings such as Fateh Khan's wedding reception, where Habshi *amirs* were among the most distinguished
guests, to the Abyssinian foot soldiers of Ambar's army—was

notable; still, there existed a racial hierarchy, from which Ambar, despite his power and authority and high family connections, was not fully immune.[19]

After ten years as Nizam Shah, Sultan Murtaza II, whom Ambar had installed as a twenty-year-old, had begun to resist some of the Regent's directives. One of the Nizam Shah's senior wives, a woman of Persian descent, had, for some time, prodded him to assert a greater degree of independence. Hearing from his upset daughter—a younger wife of the Sultan—that the Persian wife called her "a mere slave girl," "concubine," and a "kaffir" (an infidel, nonbeliever), Ambar had both the Sultan and his Persian wife poisoned to death. If Ambar had any doubts about how to handle the Sultan's increasing lack of compliance, the Persian wife's comments helped to hasten what the Regent may have already been planning to do: Replace the Sultan with a younger member of his family. With the death of the Sultan, Ambar promptly installed the former sultan's five-year-old son as Burhan Nizam Shah III. Ambar's *de facto* rule would continue uninterrupted.[20]

Just as Persians were pitted against Abyssinians and Indo-Turkic Deccanis around notions of racial superiority/inferiority—as during the outburst by Prince Murad's general during the peace talks of 1595 about the "crows and kites" or the imprudent comments by the Nizam Shah's Persian wife toward Ambar's daughter—so too were women set against each other. Wives, for instance, were regularly set against their *saukan*, "co-wife" contenders. The infighting between the Nizam Shah's more senior Persian wife and Ambar's daughter, the Sultan's younger wife, an Abyssinian like her father, while political (as it was fundamentally about the senior wife attempting a power play through her husband) was also directed as a personal attack. Ambar, however, like his daughter (by virtue of coming to her powerful father) would not tolerate the Persian wife attempting to exert her relative race privilege (Persians being those affiliated with the ruling classes of both the Mughal Empire and the Deccani sultanates, versus Abyssinians, most of whom came to South Asia as slaves, even though some rose through the ranks to become *amirs*, noblemen). But in the context of Ambar's Regency the Persian wife was not in the superior position and paid the obvious consequences for her provocation—for race, like gender, is a function of power. Here, the Abyssinian Regent Ambar had the power to dispose of the Persian (and her husband) with no apparent opposition or consequences to himself or his daughter. It was a reversal of otherwise existing hierarchies in much of the Indian Ocean world.

The Dutchman Pieter van den Broecke recounts the events as such:

> At a certain time it happened that the king's wife, who was a white Persian woman, scolded the daughter of the aforementioned Melick Ambahaer with many bitter words, saying that she was only a kaffir woman and a concubine of the king and that her father had been a rebel against the king. The daughter informed her father of this through someone else, and her father then became so angry that he began to plot the murder of the king. He persuaded Mier Abdel Fatj [Amir 'Abd al-Fath], the king's secretary, to join him, and the latter poisoned the king a short time later with a potion. The king died immediately, leaving a young son whom Mellick Ambaer captured. He then proceeded to bring the whole country under his command. The king's son is now already twelve years old; he was only five when his father died. The Mellick goes to greet him solemnly twice each week as a token of his obedience . . . The queen who was the cause of this evil history was also poisoned, shortly after the king.[21]

Like race, certain notions of gender were ingrained and performed in a number of ways in the Deccan—from peasants in the countryside to princesses in the forts and palaces. With regards to gender, the songs of peasant women may have echoed patterns in the lives of even some of the region's most privileged women, including Ambar's daughter and her Persian *saukan*. Sung in the lyrical Dakhini of the western Deccan, women's devotional songs not only helped to popularize Islam but also reinforced specific gendered hierarchical social practices. Here the *saukan* is a "devil," obstructing the other wife's progress. Meanwhile, men, the "murshids" ("teachers"), "direct" the lives of women:

> [Be] careful in grinding,
> The devil is my *saukan*
> Which prevents me from working and tires me.
> *Ya bismillah*, hu hu *Allah* . . .
> The name of Allah comes from *alif*.
> Know that *pirs* and *murshids* can direct our lives.
> Grind the flour and sift it.
> *Ya bismillah*, hu hu *Allah* . . .[22]

Despite the extraordinary figure of Chand Bibi, or courtly women who were behind-the-scenes kingmakers (or unmakers)—including Jahangir's mother and Ambar's daughter—most women did not hold the official reins of power. Their influence was exercised and felt in other, indirect ways. For Ambar, whose influence was both direct *and* indirect, power was a means to an end—principally, to maintain the Deccan's independence and, in particular, the integrity of the Nizam Shahi by defending it to his very "last breath."[23] If he deemed an action necessary, he could be ruthless. For him, war took many forms—on the battlefield, in the court, and at home. It justified whatever actions were taken within such a context. This included imprisoning one's rival (even though both were fighting the same enemy), poisoning the *saukan* of one's daughter (even though they shared a husband), and even murdering the sultan to whom one had publicly pledged one's allegiance. In these ways, perhaps, Ambar was no different from his enemies in their respective quests for power, prestige, or, as it were, simple human vengeance.

CHAPTER 6

BARGI-GIRI, DIPLOMACY, AND DEFENSE

LIKE A WAVE RIPPLING OVER the dusty landscape, one thousand warriors on their knees—Habshi, Deccani, and Persian alike—bowed in the remnants of light glowing just over the horizon. There, facing west, toward Mecca, they performed *Salat-al-Maghrib*, the prayer immediately following sunset. It was a rare moment in which Malik Ambar's enemies could breathe a sigh of relief during the wars he waged against them. As Ambar struck at all hours, and fiercely, including with "fiery missiles (*átash-bázi*)" followed by cavalry raids, those who opposed him could hardly rest—a critical aspect of guerrilla warfare.[1] During *namaz* (prayer), and armed only with their faith—swords sheathed and placed aside—Ambar's Muslim combatants were indistinguishable. Neither rank, nor race, nor age could be discerned among them; and never too far were their Hindu brothers-in-arms, the Maratha cavalry, circling around, on guard, like the Oromo mounted warriors of Ambar's youth—now a world and a lifetime away.

The respected Mughal envoy Mirza Asad Beg, who was sent to the Deccan to strengthen imperial relations, personally observed Ambar's encampments. Describing the Abyssinian leader in his memoirs as "a brave and discreet man," he went on to note, "One of his qualities was that in his camp every night twelve thousand men recited the Holy Qur'an. He offered his prayers with the common people whose number was never less than a thousand. His charities are beyond description."[2] Yet Ambar was principally a man of war, not a saint, who took ruthless action when necessary as part of his political and military command. Nonetheless, he did not distance himself from those he ruled. As Beg attests, he regularly connected with "the common people" and served them with great generosity.

Outside of the serenity of *namaz*, Ambar was dealing with almost constant attack and discord around him. Attending to any number of political and military imperatives at any one time, the conditions under which he was operating and the expectations he had created for himself required that he do so. With armies attacking from the north, internal dissent, assassination attempts, and opposition by his on-again, off-again Bijapuri and Golconda allies, Ambar might have sought solace in his religion and faith, perhaps recalling in his more vulnerable moments the Qur'anic injunction to "Seek help in patience and prayer for Allah is with those who are patient (*as-sabirin*)" (Sura 2:153). As with other combatants, prayer may have offered him relief, taking him to another place, another space, somewhere where he too could breathe more easily, if only for a few moments in the midst of war.

Ambar's patience surely played a part in reclaiming the Fort of Ahmednagar in 1610, when his forces finally ousted the Mughals from that single, though symbolically important, garrison. Emboldened by a string of victories against the imperialists, Ambar moved his capital once again, this time even farther north, from provincial Junnar to Daulatabad (his first headquarters, at Parenda, was much further south). The new capital was located northwest of Ahmednagar, near Khirki, which he developed as a model city. Daulatabad, however, had historical weight, being a former seat of the Delhi Sultanate's Tughluq dynasty, whose rebel general Hasan Gangu (dubbed Bahman Shah) had led a revolt in the northern Deccan three centuries earlier.

Time, it seems, was on Ambar's side; his faith, deep and abiding, seems to have shielded and comforted him. But as a rebel leader, administrator, and diplomat, Ambar was both a master tactician and strategist, and therefore highly pragmatic. As a general and statesman he tended to think and act with a long-term view, and in this way, he was at once disciplined and flexible, where some of his enemies tended to be either rash or rigid, or both. Like the deciduous trees of the western Deccan, Ambar knew how to bend with the wind and shed his pride when necessary. His own "intelligence" would include an extensive network of spies throughout the sultanate to ensure that he had the very best information to make whatever decisions were necessary. As Shyam notes, "He never failed to obtain the fullest and minutest information about the movements of the enemy, its strength and its weak points."[3]

Undogmatic but firm, Ambar appears to have been driven by different senses of urgency and sources of inspiration, material and metaphysical alike. The result gave him an air of invincibility and served as a source of ongoing frustration for those who opposed him. For some, however, his narrow escapes from being captured on the battlefield were not proof of divine grace but of the devil's work. The Italian nobleman and visitor to the Deccan Pietro della Valle was told by some of Ambar's detractors that the Abyssinian was "addicted to sorcery [which is how he] keeps himself in favour with his king." According to these stories, "works of Inchantments" were responsible for his success. But they went further, accusing Ambar of the "most horrid impieties and cruelties, killing hundreds of his slaves' children and others, and offering them as sacrifice to the invoked devils." Yet, the Italian concludes of these and "other abominable stories which I have heard related [that] because not seen by myself, I affirm not for true."[4]

Whether through divine intervention, magic, or serendipity, Ambar's surviving multiple assassination attempts surely gave pause to those who tried but repeatedly failed to kill him. In 1612

Ambar signed an important treaty with the Mughals, which continued to hold, albeit uneasily. For the moment, at least, secure from overt imperial attack and with his handpicking of yet another and even younger Nizam Shah, Ambar's power and authority within the sultanate appeared supreme. Soon, however, jealousies flared and intrigues formed around him. Complaints among some commanders about Ambar's heavy-handed rule simmered beneath the relative calm across the land. Among those opposing Ambar were several Rajput officers under his command. The proud descendants of northern Hindu warriors, the Rajputs' issue was not one of religion, but the degree to which Ambar wielded power and authority.

Among the several known attempts on Ambar's life was one by a group of his Rajput officers in 1613. Describing the assassination attempt, Emperor Jahangir's court chronicler Mu'tamad Khan writes that "the Rajputs who had resolved to kill Ambar had concealed themselves till they found the opportunity of approaching him, when one of them gave him an effectual wound. The men in the escort of Ambar killed the Rajputs, and carried their master off home." Khan ends by noting, "A very little more would [have] made an end of this cursed fellow."[5] Cursed by some, praised by others, Ambar survived this and all other assassination attempts—including those of 1614 by a group of Nizam Shahi chiefs as well as agents of Ibrahim Adil Shah II in 1621 and 1624. (One can only imagine how many unrecorded assassination attempts were made by *Mughal* agents over the years.)[6]

Kismet (destiny) aside, Ambar's survival and success were also the result of his disciplined military organization and battlefield tactics. Next to the Mughals, whose peace of 1612 ended two years later, Ambar's forces were almost always outmanned and outgunned. Although there were certain times in which his forces outnumbered those of the Mughals—when, for instance, he mustered the considerable combined support of the sultanates of Bijapur and Golconda—Ambar and his commanders were mostly at a disadvantage in terms of canons, munitions, elephants, and foot soldiers—the generals' pawns. But what Ambar lacked in numbers and weight, he made up with speed and agility—namely, his lightning-quick Maratha cavalry force, the cutting edge of his army. For the most part, he avoided pitched battles in open fields in favor of quick engagements in uneven terrain with attacks on enemy supply lines and encampments. As Tamaskar describes, "Generally, he chose his time carefully, made the necessary preparations and dealt blows on the enemy suddenly and struck hard . . . He knew when to bend and when to strike."[7]

Ambar seems to have mastered certain aspects of *bargi-giri* (guerrilla warfare) early in the war against the Mughals. Just after the turn of the century Mughal court chroniclers wrote, "At Mulkapur, a great fight took place with Malik Ambar . . . the imperialists, unaccustomed to the warfare of the Dak'hinis, lost heavily."[8] Abu'l Fazl wrote, "Ambar Jīū [a variation on the name "Chapu"] attacked with a large force of Deccanis and Abyssinians . . . He made little fight and then retired . . . that evil disposed Abyssinian [Malik Ambar] collected a number of presumptuous men, and the prosperity of the rebellious increased."[9] Still another imperial account notes:

> The enemy [Ambar] kept a sharp watch over his [the Mughal general 'Abdu-llah Khan's] movements, and sent a large force of Mahrattas (*bargiyán*), who skirmished with him all day, and harassed him at night . . . Ambar the black-faced, who had placed himself in command of the enemy, continually brought up reinforcements till he had assembled a large force, and he constantly annoyed 'Abdu-llah [Khan] with rockets and various kinds of fiery missiles (*átash-bázi*), till he reduced him to a sad condition . . . it was deemed expedient to retreat, and prepare for a new campaign.[10]

European travelers who accompanied Mughal expeditions into the Deccan noted several embarrassing defeats by Ambar's much smaller forces. Joannes De Laet, a Flemish geographer and philologist who worked at the Mughal court and later became a director of the Dutch East India Company, recalled how in 1611 Ambar resisted joint armies, the first commanded by General Khan Jahan Lodi and the second by the Governor of Gujarat Abdullah Khan. De Laet writes, "The plan was that the two forces would meet at Daulatabad and attack [Malik Ambar], the minister of Ahmednagar, but Abdullah Khan ... arrived early and was harassed by the guerilla bands (Bargis) of the Nizam Shahi minister." Here, Ambar seized upon the lack of discipline among the imperialists' leadership, which was prone to impulsive action, including (as in this case) the Mughal general Lodi overestimating his armies' strength by trying to grab the glory of defeating Ambar without waiting for the second army to be in position to attack. De Laet goes on to describe Ambar's other military successes, including capturing "the provinces of Candhees and Baraer."[11]

Although Ambar was helped by the undisciplined military actions of some Mughal leaders, his success in defending the Deccan was also a function of his long-term planning: military recruitment, training, and the maintenance of a chain of fortifications across the land and on the coast. One of the most important ways Ambar kept watch over his enemies' movements was through the forts. While Ambar was less active in building new forts during his rule, he expanded, structurally reinforced, and maintained those that already dotted the vast countryside of the western Deccan and the region's western seaboard. The forts of Galna, Junnar, Daulatabad, Ahmednagar, Parenda, Mahur, Sholapur, Morro, and Janjira were among the over forty geographically spread fortifications that enabled Ambar to guard the realm against repeated attacks over the course of two and a half decades.

At times, some of Ambar's forts were taken, such as Ahmednagar—which was retaken by his Deccani forces before going back into Mughal possession. Most, however, remained firmly in his hands. The siege warfare used to capture forts could sometimes last for months at a time. The long stretches required additional munitions and the renewal of fresh supplies (food and water) for soldiers, horses, and elephants. War elephants, critical to sieges, were loaded with light cannon and guns and used in battering the walls of fortresses. During Ambar's time the French navigator François Pyrard de Laval, who visited the Nizam Shahi on his way back from the Maldives, noted that the sultanate had a "large number of elephants" as part of its army.[12] Such elephants were actively sought by Ambar, as when the *Akbarnama* carefully records that Ambar captured fourteen war elephants from Bidar and then twenty-nine elephants from Golconda during the early stages of the protracted war against the Mughals—that is, when he was asserting his authority in the region.[13]

In undermining a siege, as in the siege of the Fort of Ahmednagar, among others, Ambar proved particularly adept at disrupting Mughal supply lines and raiding them for his armies' use. Mughal supply lines feeding their large and slow-moving armies were invariably weaker at the margins and more vulnerable to Ambar's *bargi-giri*. Siege warfare, however, was a critical part of establishing territorial boundaries and therefore critical to the Nizam Shahi, for which Ambar had primary political responsibility.

Whether Ambar's troops were defending one of their own forts against a siege or laying siege to a fort themselves, the support of the people was vital. For the capture of forts and fortifications, *hasham* (infantry) was necessary, but so was winning the hearts and minds of those in the countryside—those who ultimately fed the armies and could aid them in particularly troubled times. Ambar's popular support was therefore an essential part of his ability to defend and take offensive action. We get a sense of Ambar's wider support in Ferishta's observation that the "Khan-Khanan [Mughal commander-in-chief], well aware of [Malik Ambar's] enterprising character and popularity in the country, feared the Moghuls might be *eventually* overpowered" [emphasis added].[14]

Equally important for Ambar was winning over the Deccan's large number of Maratha warriors, and in particular its cavalrymen (and perhaps some women who entered in disguise). Relying heavily on his cavalry force, the pride of Maratha horsemanship, Ambar tended not to use as many foot soldiers in his army as other Deccani powers, and certainly not the Mughals. Outside of siege warfare, only in critical circumstances did he call for battle leading with foot soldiers—as the numbers rarely favored him. Nevertheless, Ambar did use infantry; as Shyam notes, late in Ambar's career, for instance, "while fighting against the Portuguese at Ravadanda he requisitioned 100 foot-soldiers (*hasham*) from the *karkoons* of Chaul."[15]

Ambar seldom engaged in conventional warfare where two armies met in an open field and attacked each other. Typically, in the quiet but tense prelude to such battles, if one of the armies did not back down, a shot was fired, signaling the start of the engagement. A round of artillery meant to break up and thin out enemy lines would be followed by a hail of arrows. During one battle with the Mughals in Qandahar, the gun smoke was so thick—with arrows "whizzing" past Ambar's soldiers—that the imperial chronicler Abu'l-Fazl describes how "From the smoke of guns and muskets . . . day put on the dark robes of night."[16] When the air cleared archers aimed to pierce light armor with the hope of hitting spaces unprotected by chainmail. Infantry would then battle it out in a slaughter of hand-to-hand combat before elephants and cavalry charged, adding to the destruction. Whichever army was able to hold its position longest was the nominal victor. In war, winning meant little more than the claim of having done so, with the aftermath of such battles being scenes of horror—with the cries of the injured eventually dying out, the bodies and parts of warriors and animals strewn across the blood-drenched soil.

Given both the Mughal's numerically superior forces and the rugged terrain of the western Deccan, cavalry was of better use in defending the Deccan than infantry. Toward this end, Ambar appointed a separate commander-in-chief for his cavalry force. Siddi Yakub Khan, an Abyssinian, was given this important charge and reported directly to Ambar. Khan had apparently proven his leadership capacities among the Maratha and perhaps served as one of Ambar's confidants (that is, someone who walked with him). Such high-ranking officers were necessarily close to Ambar. These officers included a number of Maratha commanders whom he entrusted with his authority and whom he held in high esteem (Ambar would name several districts of Khirki after his Maratha generals). Ambar's particular attention to Maratha military leadership in the Deccan was a glowing feature of his rule; in turn, Maratha joined the Abyssinian minister's guerrilla army in increasing numbers.

The steady growth of Ambar's Maratha cavalry, which more than doubled in size about every decade, appears to have been done in a very deliberate way. While his cavalry consisted of fewer than four thousand in 1600, by 1609 he had enlarged it to ten thousand; by 1624, it is estimated that Ambar had fifty thousand Maratha cavalrymen under his command. When recruiting new Maratha he trained them in the quick-striking techniques he had refined from battle tactics already in existence in the region. Describing the maneuvers of Ambar's Maratha light cavalry, Shyam notes how they "engaged in hovering on the right and the left flanks of the enemy, cutting off their lines of communication, intercepting their supplies, seizing their provisions and delivering surprise attacks on their camps in the night." Sweeping in at full speed, "the Maratha *bargis* would in the first instance fight the enemy and then disappear in different directions and collect again and take the enemy by surprise." Ambar's cavalry was particularly deadly during the rainy season, swarming into enemy camps and causing chaos while remaining organized themselves.[17] As one scholar puts it, Ambar essentially "waged a war of movement rather than of sieges."[18]

For Ambar, defending the Deccan sometimes meant taking particular offensive action—that is, even going into Mughal territory or lands over which the Emperor had suzerainty. In 1609, an English contemporary observed how Ambar attacked Surat (in Gujarat): "Malik Ambar, a noble of Nizam'sah's court . . . invaded Gujarat at the head of 50,000 horse and plundered, and [then] retired, as quickly as he came." The next year he laid siege to the Mughal headquarters at Burhanpur, and in 1620 he even attacked Malwa beyond the Marmada. But even as Ambar sometimes carried war into Mughal land, he was also flexible, conceding nominal victory on his own land to the imperialists for strategic purposes. As Shyam notes:

> It is true that Prince Shah Jahan won victory twice over [Ambar] but his success on both the occasions was more [for show] than real. In spite of his superiority of numbers and resources he failed to seize even an inch of territory or a single fort from the hands of Malik Ambar . . . Each time, no sooner did the prince turn his back than Malik Ambar started the counter offensive, driving the enemy across the Narbada [river] and recovering his losses.[19]

While securing land, Ambar also built an alliance with Habshi sailors who had taken control of and built the formidable island fortress of Janjira just off the coast of the Sultanate of Ahmednagar. The populations on the western coast of India had seen a number of Abyssinians gain prominence going back at least a century before Ambar's rule—with a wider presence across the western Indian Ocean world going back many centuries earlier. As observers from the ninth-century Ethiopian-Iraqi literary figure Al-Jahiz to the fourteenth-century North African jurist and traveler Ibn Battuta variously noted, black warriors were a visible part of many of the kingdoms of the western Indian Ocean world—the latter describing Abyssinians as "the guarantors of safety" on the Indian Ocean.[20] Some of these seafaring Africans came to hold significant power and leadership positions on India's western seaboard. For instance, in 1530, Sayf al-Mulk Miftah, described as an Ethiopian, was the governor of Daman on the coast of Ahmednagar, commanding a force of 4,000 Habshi soldiers.[21]

Janjira, derived from the word *jazeera*, meaning "island" in Arabic, was one among several key forts either built or overtaken by Abyssinians on the western coast of India. Janjira, perhaps the most impressive of the forts along the coast, was built on a rocky island at the mouth of the Bay of Rajapuri leading into the Kundalika River. It was one of over a dozen forts, largely on the mainland, controlling sea access from Daman in the north to just south of Goa. Beginning in the early seventeenth century, Habshi sailors-turned-rulers established a royal lineage at Janjira that reigned for the next three centuries. During Ambar's time, the Nizam Shahi controlled several seaports with accompanying forts along the Konkan coast, including Chaul, Dabhol, and Janjira. In 1621 Ambar, who made the backwaters of the island a base for his naval fleet, appointed Sidi Ambar, known as Sainak ("The Little"—to distinguish him from Malik Ambar) as *subhedar* (governor) of Janjira.[22]

Ambar's military planning, construction of forts and rein-forcement of existing ones, intelligence gathering, use of both conventional and guerrilla warfare, and ongoing recruitment and training of soldiers were complemented by his diplomatic skills as a statesman. He understood the importance of diplo-macy when possible and force when necessary. Moreover, as his relationships with Deccani leaders, Mughal envoys, European traders, and both Maratha and Abyssinians attest, he dealt with a range of constituencies.

Part of Ambar's diplomatic strategy was making long-term political investments, including creating family connections. In 1608 he negotiated an alliance with Sultan Ibrahim II of Bijapur in the south in order to concentrate his efforts in battling the Mughals to the north. As Eaton writes, "His efforts paid off, for just two years later, the Mughal garrison in Ahmednagar would fall and the Habshi *peshwa* would be emboldened to move the Nizam Shahi court from Junnar further north, to Daulatabad."[23] But be-cause Ambar was equally concerned about the long term he also worked to build more lasting kinship ties with Bijapur by having his son Fateh Khan marry the Adil Shah's daughter in 1609. Such relationships could and would help at future times when Ambar needed to draw upon Bijapur's assistance or mitigate against attacks from Bijapur itself.

Ambar's recorded interactions with the Mughal envoy Asad Beg, a Mughal ally named Hasan Ali Beg, and the Dutch trader Pieter van den Broecke testify to his diplomatic handling of people, which he seems to have done at a personal level, in warm ways, and, at times, with extraordinary fanfare. Asad Beg describes a particular dinner reception held by Ambar at Balaghat in the envoy's honor:

> All the amirs, members of the government, men of letters, religious leaders, and saints formed an assemblage even one tenth of which was to be rarely seen at one place in India. Religious discourses and recitals from the Qur'an were held on a scale only to be witnessed in the holy town of Mashad . . . Between the two prayers a magnificent dinner party was held, which in the Deccani dialect is called "Kanduri." A large tent was pitched in an open space, and round it were *Shamiyanas* [ceremonial awnings] decorated with the figures of fish woven into the covering. In every corner were placed brass and silver vessels, one on the top of the other to [the] height of a man, each filled with dainty eatables. Every item of food was tastily cooked, sprinkled with a profusion of spices. There were numerous varieties of delicious puddings, sweets, cakes, unleavened bread, all beyond praise, description or exaggeration.[24]

The opulence of the reception is reminiscent of a description by the Portuguese Francisco Álvares of the sprawling imperial encampments in Ethiopia—which he described as "a city in a great plain," filled with colorful pavilions—and speaks to Ambar's power, prominence, and influence.

Such was the wealth of the ruling classes of India, which often set the stage for important talks. Following the formal part of the reception, Asad Beg asked Ambar to join him in breaching a misunderstanding with a Mughal ally. Following the great reception, "the two retired into the [*sic*] privacy and laid bare their inmost thoughts in an open-hearted talk . . . and both of them parted company with each other as friends," writes Asad Beg.[25] But Ambar treated Mughals in "friendly" terms for tactical purposes. After all, the Mughals were fundamentally his enemy, no matter how kindly and openly he appeared to treat any one of their representatives or allies.

Diplomacy without the backing of force, however, was ultimately limited in its effect. Ambar was repeatedly left fighting without the support of, or sometimes even under direct attack by, other Deccani sultanates. At several points in his career he was in fact placed in the position of having to appear as if he had capitulated to the Mughals as a way of buying more time, sometimes simply to give his soldiers time to rest, or as a way of opening up new political opportunities. Ambar started one set of negotiations with the Mughals after being defeated in battle by sending his agents and officers to his victor, Prince Shah Jahan, with requests that "after this I will not drop the thread of service and loyalty from my hand nor put out my foot beyond and will regard whatever tribute and fine be commanded as favour and will send it to the government." It was a humiliating peace but one that was necessary since the rulers of Bijapur and Golconda were not willing to back him up; in fact, they often used Ambar as a safety valve in order to protect their own immediate interests.[26]

Not unlike the friendly manner in which Ambar dealt with the Mughals, his meeting with the Dutchman van den Broecke illustrates the Regent Minister's personal and warm disposition—someone with a keen sense of humor. Van den Broecke, who later became the manager of the Dutch East India Company at Surat, in Gujarat (under Mughal control), observed in 1617 Ambar's diplomatic handling of various figures and personalities as the Regent received ambassadors and Portuguese renegades and met with the Dutch merchant himself:

*Pieter van den Broecke, oil on canvas by the Haarlem-
based Dutch artist Frans Hals, circa 1633.*

I went in person to the Melick Ambahaer, bringing as presents a
Japanese saber and an expensive Javanese kris [dagger]. [He] gave
me also a permit for the rest of our people, was very friendly, and
hung two expensive *pomerins* [colored cloths] around my shoulders, one made of gold, the other one of camel's hair; this is the
greatest honor one can give a person. He also offered to give me
soldiers as a guard and convoy to Golconda.

He had with him an ambassador . . . who requested his horse back
and compensations for damages done to his people. I told Melick
Ambaer that I was now in his land and under his authority; that
I had come to his land trusting his word, since he is considered in
the whole world as a man who scrupulously keeps his word. If it
was his wish that I return the horse, then I would give it up, but not

of my free will, indeed very much against it. But if this was not his wish, then [the] soldiers should try to get it by force of arms. He began to laugh and gave the message to the ambassador, who did not like it a bit.

In our company were also some Portuguese *arnegados* [renegades] who said, in Portuguese, "Look at that proud dog," *Vede iste suberbe can!* They came to the Melick to request command of 3, 4, or 5,000 horses. They said: "This dog only comes to spy; watch out." With a friendly face he gave my leave and I rode back to my tent.

Describing Ambar's command, conviction, and composure, Van den Broeke's eyewitness account provides a rare glimpse into the daily affairs of the Abyssinian, then at the height of his power in the Deccan. These lighter interactions, however, would have been fleeting moments in an otherwise grinding war with little end in sight. Still, like those moments of *namaz*, they existed, helping to relieve the mind, if not the soul.

CHAPTER 7

| THE PEOPLE AND THE BATTLE |
OF BHATVADI

ACROSS THE LAND, HUTS MADE of woven reed plastered with mud served as the homes of the men and women who lived outside of the towering forts and marble-lined palaces of those who ruled over them. Vulnerable to the vagaries of war, the whims of the powerful, and the ever-present possibility of drought, India's peasants—from small children to village elders—worked the soil that grew the food that fed the soldiers, the nobles, and the sultans who regularly ran roughshod over them. As elsewhere in the world, the wealth and leisure of those who ruled—from the Mughal emperors and their vassals, to the sultans and ministers of the Deccan—rested on the men and women who bowed and bent beneath the burden of it all.[1]

Whether in the Ethiopia of Ambar's youth or the India of his older age, peasant farmers across the Indian Ocean world were driven by the thought of famine or the threat of force. Sometimes, however, rulers drew their respect and not just their fear. In the Deccan, as in northern India, peasants were careful not to incur the wrath of those who would further exploit them; nevertheless, like all subjugated people, they actively resisted the demands of the state and their overlords in hidden ways. As the anthropologist James C. Scott writes, "So long as we confine our conception of *the political* to activity that is openly declared we are driven to

83

conclude that subordinate groups essentially lack a political life." He continues, "To do so is to miss the immense political terrain that lies between quiescence and revolt . . . It is to focus on the visible coastline of politics and miss the continent that lies beyond."[2]

Beyond India's long coastline, the Deccan would include tens of millions of people whose lives went unrecorded or underrecorded by Mughal and Deccani court chroniclers. If they did appear in written accounts, they did so in passing or in relation to the quantity of crops they produced. We nevertheless hear some of their voices through the *chakki-nama* and *charkha-nama*—songs women sang while working. These "grinding" and "spinning" songs sung by women while spinning cotton and grinding grain into flour have been passed down from one generation to the next. From one *charkha-nama*, the words "The tongue is the unspun thread for the message of Allah . . . Bring out the thread of breath and show it, Oh Sister," although written by men to infuse Islam into local communities, may have been understood as an affirmation of women's *own* sacred voice. And while there is little documentary evidence of women's resistance to existing or imposed inequitable gender practices in the Deccan, we have some sense of the ways in which both they and their male counterparts resisted the unjust policies and practices imposed upon them by their shared rulers. Perhaps the most common form of *political* resistance took the form of economic sabotage—that is, working less efficiently or underreporting crop yields.[3]

Peasants cultivated food grains, such as millet, rice, and wheat, as well as oilseeds, fibers, and spices, and to a smaller extent grew gardens for additional household consumption and bartering goods. Animal rearing supplemented the main agricultural activities, but the cultivation of crops was the basis of economic prosperity in the region. War and droughts, however, loomed large among peasant communities. Calamity befell the region's poor when crops were either taken or destroyed by soldiers. With similar devastating effect, when droughts hit, hunger threatened. Under such conditions peasant communities were left susceptible to epidemics that swept through the countryside like storms of locusts.[4]

While peasants in the Deccan lived materially difficult lives, they probably also had moments of storytelling, laughter, and joy, the creation of music, art, and dance, as well as words of wisdom, poetry, and playful tricks. That is, amidst the destruction of war and in the face of hunger—elements that often and tragically drove people from their villages—peasants lived their lives and loved their children. In addition to the mass of peasant farmers, there were artisans, carpenters, blacksmiths, saddlers, potters, and a range of servants. Subjects paid taxes in the form of crops (artisans were often supported by the village as a whole in exchange for their services, while servant's masters were responsible for their taxes); over the course of the seventeenth century, cash payment came to be required along with crops. Each group of fifty to two hundred villages had their own bazaars (marketplaces) and formed a *pargana* ("district")—the main administrative unit of the sultanate.[5]

Whatever their particular skill or trade, the basis of life was agriculture—and the basis of agriculture was careful water management. When the rains came, crops grew in abundance and peasants could eat and pay their taxes; when the rains failed, their lives were especially harsh, even destitute. There are stories of people eating grass to fill their bellies, wandering the countryside in search of food, and even selling themselves and their loved ones to wealthy landowners out of desperation. Famine haunted the lives of peasants, just as the outbreak of diseases wiped out entire villages. But these were the worst of times. Bountiful crops also came and benefited Ambar and his class of rulers by providing the food that sustained them and their armies.

Although Ambar had won a string of bold military actions between 1607 and 1612, the period thereafter saw a change in his fortunes. Among Ambar's defeats, there was one especially devastating battle against the Mughals near Paitan in 1616. There,

Hindu saddler and female peasant, "Seventy-Two Specimens of Castes in India."

thousands of his soldiers, many very young, were killed. As the Bijapuri court chronicler Fuzuni Astarabadi recounts:

> With the Habshi nobles and the Mughal army [General Shah Nawaz Khan] marched to the bank of the [Godavari] river of Paitan. Every day Ambar's nobles used to come and fight like *bargis* . . . Spies reported to the Mughal general that Ambar himself was coming with 40,000 horses . . . The Mughals took post in a village encircled by the river . . . with a deep ditch in front, behind which they planted their artillery. The next day Ambar appeared. His squadron of *bachgan* [pages], ten thousand Habshis, of the age of 17 or 18, mounted on Persian horses, charged from the front of Ambar. They were caught by the deep ditch and could neither advance nor retreat, being huddled together as if they had been chained. In this position they were mown down by the Mughal artillery, like leaves of trees under a destroying wind . . . The Mughals then advanced to the attack, slaying many of his slaves. A great defeat and flight fell on Ambar's army . . .[6]

The battle on the banks of the Godavari River in 1616 culminated in the fall of Ahmednagar to the Mughals the following year. Nevertheless, Emperor Jahangir—increasingly frustrated, indeed crazed, by his inability to fully defeat Ambar, who conceded minor defeats while maintaining the integrity of his realm—had the artist Abu'l-Hasan paint a dream scene (a fantasy) of him killing the Abyssinian regent. A vivid image, the painting reveals the level of anxiety that Ambar produced in the emperor. Jahangir is depicted shooting an arrow at Ambar's impaled head with an owl on top perhaps representing Ambar's night raids on Mughal troops. The capture of Ahmednagar may have offered momentary relief to the increasingly unstable emperor, whose wife Nur Jahan would eventually take over the daily operations of the court in her husband's maddened absence. Meanwhile, Jahangir's son, the future Shah Jahan, launched a rebellion against his father.

Given the volatile context, Ambar shifted toward a more cautious strategy. In the Deccan, as in northern Mughal lands, allies could and would become bitter enemies, or simply rational opportunists. In terms of the Deccan, its defense had long been realized through temporary alliances between various sultanates against the Mughals; while the sultanates were never fully united, they did offer each other assistance at critical moments—indeed, Ambar demanded and received tribute to pay for his military services in defense of the Deccan, not just the Nizam Shahi. However, by 1618 it was becoming clear that the Adil Shah of Bijapur was prepared to turn his back on Ambar and the Nizman Shahi. Jahangir prodded Adil Shah to take action against the other sultanates, promising him "whatever territory" he captured. Mughal court chroniclers wrote: "A gracious *firman* was issued that [the Adil Shah] should be presented with whatever territory of Nizamu-l-mulk [Nizam Shah] or Qutub-l-mulk [Qutub Shah] he might get into his possession, and whenever he should require any support and assistance, Shah Nawaz Khan should prepare an army and appoint to assist him."[7] Despite Ambar's family ties to

Bijapuri nobility and the distant but still pertinent lesson of 1595 of not inviting the Mughals into the Deccan, Adil Shah was now entertaining the possibility of working *with* the Mughals.

Ambar was compelled to play the game of deference and supplication—a game mastered by peasants in the presence of their overlords—not only toward the Mughals but also toward his fellow Deccani sultanates, most importantly Adil Shah, who was working on a clandestine pact with the Mughals. From Ambar's standpoint, if the Nizam Shahi fell, the entire region would fall. But for the rulers of Golconda and Bijapur, they were willing to take their chances. History would judge their decision—but long before this played out, Ambar gained widespread admiration (and envy) when news spread of the outcome of what became his crowning military achievement in September 1624: the Battle of Bhatvadi.

In the five years leading up to the Battle of Bhatvadi, in which Ambar defeated the Mughals and their Deccani allies, the Adil Shah had been drifting over to the northerners to save himself for when (he believed) the imperialists, now concentrating their efforts to take over the Deccan, might become their overlords. Jahangir extended the title of *Farzand* ("son") to Adil Shah for accepting to serve him and thanked the Sultan of Bijapur by sending him a portrait of the emperor himself.[8] In early 1619, despite having agreed to a tripartite alliance with Ambar and the Portuguese against the Mughals, Ibrahim Adil Shah II sent his army to occupy Puna, the Nizam Shah's second largest city. The occupation was temporary but still an act of military aggression. Ambar remained composed, exercising restraint, but the Adil Shah became even more belligerent toward his neighboring Deccani sultanates. Without warning, he turned on the smaller Barid Shahi Sultanate to his north, marching straight into its capital and imprisoning its ruler, Ali Barid II, and his sons. Bijapur's Adil Shah II was now working alongside the Mughals to pull the Deccan apart. From this point onward, Ambar would have two fronts to protect, Jahangir to the north and Adil Shah to the south.

Tense and bitter times followed between Ambar and the Adil Shahi, with one after another skirmish leading the former to sacrifice partial territory to his enemies to both the north and south in order to protect the vital heart of the Nizam Shahi. Additional assassination attempts were directed toward Ambar, including in 1621 and 1624, with Adil Shah agents failing to kill the Regent by trying to drown him in a tank and then by trying to poison him. However, Ambar was a consummate survivor. With the foiling of these plots, the Mughals and Adil Shah conspired to attack Ambar with the combined weight of their armies.[9]

The events immediately preceding the Battle of Bhatvadi began with Ibrahim Adil Shah II sending five thousand of his best troops and officers under the command of General Mulla Muhammed Lari to escort the Mughals to Burhanpur in order to defeat Ambar. Eight years earlier, in 1616, the same Adil Shah had sent Lari with twenty thousand horses to *help* Ambar against a Mughal attack.[10] With the secret pact between the Mughals and Adil Shah now exposed to the light of day, Ambar left his capital, Khirki, and had the Nizam Shahi family removed to the nearby hill fort of Daulatabad. In the meantime, he sent a note to the imperial throne asking that the Nizam Shahi and Adil Shahi might be allowed to settle their old differences without interference. The effort was to no avail; Ambar, it was later said, "spared no effort to avoid war."[11] But Ambar was shrewd and knew that he had better strike before being struck himself.

Readying his troops, Ambar first launched an attack on Bidar, taking a Bijapuri army long stationed there by complete surprise. Before the dust had even settled in Bidar Ambar next turned his sights on Bijapur, aiming for Ibrahim Adil Shah II himself. Moving headfirst into the southern wind with his army of Abyssinian-Maratha-Deccani warriors at his back, Ambar stormed and lay siege to the capital. Adil Shah had taken refuge in the fort and asked the Mughals to come to his rescue. Outmanned by what was now a triple alliance of Mughal, Adil Shah, and Qutub Shah against him, Ambar returned to his kingdom and prepared

for a confrontation with armies headed by, among others, Ikhlas
Khan and Mulla Muhammed Lari, whom the contemporary Italian observer Pietro della Valle had described as a leading
warmonger.[12]

Ambar carefully picked the area near the village of Bhatvadi
as the battle site. Located ten miles southeast of Ahmednagar in a
hilly tract on the western bank of the Kalinadi, a small feeder of
the Sina River, it was an ideal location for the guerrilla tactics that
he would need to employ against numerically superior forces. The
Battle of Bhatvadi began on September 10, 1624 (1033 A.H.).
Fuzuni Astarabadi, the Persian Adil Shahi court chronicler, provides a vivid account:

> Ambar marched away towards his own dominions. Adil Shah sent
> a large force under Ikhlas Khan Habshi on the heels of Ambar . . .
> so that this army [advanced] from the front and Mulla Muham-
> mad from behind. Ambar seeing himself surrounded by the tem-
> pest of calamity, left the road and with a few soldiers entered the
> strong fort of Bhatvadi, and gave repose to his soldiers. By [letting
> out] the water of the lake of Bhatvadi, he barred the path before the
> Mughal army [and] the abundance of mud and mire weakened the
> Mughal army, and though his own men were fewer, his heart re-
> mained confident in reliance upon Allah . . .
>
> The rainy season invested the ground with the mantle of water; the
> excess of mud and rain weakened both the armies. Scarcity of food
> reached an extreme point in the camps of the Mughals and Adil
> Shah. For two or three nights together the quadrupeds did not get
> any fodder; what could the men get? Things came to such a pass that
> strength for movement was not left in the bodies of men or beasts.
>
> At Mulla Muhammad's request, Adil Shah sent treasure and provi-
> sions, but the convoy after arriving near the frontier did not dare
> proceed further in fear of Ambar's troops. At this time, as in the
> Mughal army the soldiers did not get their pay and there was no

food, many went over to Ambar-jiu, who welcomed, honored and fed them and took them into his service.

[Ten] thousand [of Ambar's] horsemen strong . . . delivered a night attack on the Mughal camp, and came back to their place in the morning. This occurred repeatedly. Terror of Ambar's army seized the hearts of the enemies' troops, they spent their nights without sleep and their days without repose. Matters at last came to such a pass, that when Mulla Muhammad ordered any officer to go out and escort the treasure and provisions, nobody would agree to do it, in terror . . .

Ambar's strength daily increased and that of the Mughals decreased, till at last he gave up night-attacks and began to wage battles by day. On many days coming from one side he would plunder and slay a party and go back . . . At last Ambar planted his own tent and the Nizam Shahi royal standard (*nah-gazi*) in front of the Mughal army with great pomp and demonstration . . .

A great disgrace fell upon the armies of the three [allied] kings . . . Malik Ambar swollen to greatness by this victory, from an ant into a snake, [was] enriched with wealth exceeding the treasures of Corah, and troops numerous beyond imagination.[13]

By dictating the battle site, flooding the grounds, disrupting enemy supply lines, and launching repeated night attacks, Ambar systematically wore down his opponents—so much so that many Mughals soldiers came to his side, whom he wisely welcomed with open arms. To the imperial forces' surprise, Ambar had used water, the life source of the land, to sound their own death-knell. With each desertion to his side, his forces grew stronger. In the end, the combined Mughal, Adil Shahi, and Qutub Shahi armies sustained a crushing defeat.

Among the many men killed in battle was Mulla Muhammad Lari (knocked off his horse by a projectile rumored to have been shot by someone on his own side); among those taken prisoner was Ikhlas Khan. Ambar's masterful defense of the Nizam Shahi would become legendary. If ever there was an example of his military genius, this was it; but, as in all things, his success was more than just his own individual making. Ambar, whose son Fateh Khan fought alongside him, was supported by a number of great *sardars* (leaders) at Bhatvadi, in particular his Maratha commanders. Among them were Shahaji Raje Bhosale—the son of Ambar's long-trusted officer Maloji Raje Bhosale (who died two years earlier) and the future father of the great Maratha leader Shivaji (born two and a half years later).

Although soldiers were both the immediate perpetrators *and* victims of war, such as those young Habshi soldiers who had fallen "like leaves of trees under a destroying wind," as Fuzuni Astarabadi described the ill-fated battle of 1616, peasants and townspeople were regularly victimized as armies swept through their villages.[14] For instance, the Qutub Shahi court chronicler Sayyid Tabataba writes of events in Paithan, south of Khirki: "[The Mughals] marched to the town of Paithan [and with] some of the poorest and feeblest of the inhabitants of the country, trusting to the general amnesty, had remained in the town, began to plunder all the houses therein and violently despoiled those people of all the valuable stuffs, money and goods, even going so far as to strip both men and women of their clothes, leaving not a covering for women, gentle or simple."[15]

We get further sense of the destruction of invading and occupying Mughal armies on the Deccani people through other commentaries—for instance, when the Abyssinian nobleman Shamshir Khan Habshi denounced Miyan Manjhu Dakhni, who had invited the Mughals into the region and left "the plains of the dominion and all the subjects to be trampled upon by the enemy's army."[16] Several years later, moreover, as the chronicler Ferishta distressingly observes, it "became a custom for the Ahmednagar army to take the fields twice a year ... to devastate and plunder the country contiguous to Daulatabad, in order, if possible, to reduce it by famine."[17]

The devastation of war and the ransacking and pillaging of town and country by unrestrained soldiers, combined with droughts and ensuing famine, were compounded by the exploitative practices of those in positions of power and authority. As Ferishta notes of events at the Fort of Parenda in 1603, "the governor's son having committed some cruelty on the inhabitants of the place, they rebelled and slew him, and his father was himself compelled to fly."[18] Injustices and corruption were then, as now, part of the lived experiences of ordinary people. More specific to the region, the large Hindu population of Maharashtra, which covered much of the northern Deccan, was organized around an ancient hierarchical caste system. As with other social, religious, and political systems, the Hindu caste system included systemic forms of corruption—and like the Sufis who took jabs at the hierarchies created within Islamic societies, injustices to the poor were protested by poets who came from Hindu communities.

Among the best-known Hindu poets of the Deccan during the latter part of Ambar's life was a Bakhti spiritualist named Sant Tukaram. Born into a merchant family near Puna within the Nizam Shahi, Tukaram gave poignant poetic expression to the ways in which the Deccan's poor were mistreated by the powerful and privileged. In the Hindu caste hierarchy, Tukaram and his family were considered *sudra*, a large category incorporating a number of different groups and occupying a position somewhere between the Brahmin upper caste and the so-called untouchables of the lowest-caste Dalit (derived from the Sanskrit *dalita*, meaning "oppressed"). Challenging both the hierarchy of caste distinctions and their divisiveness, Tukaram states in one of his poems, "The *brahmin* who flies into a rage at the touch of a *mahar* [a member of a lower caste], that's no *brahmin*." In the same vein, he would also challenge the political corruption of the upper caste and their abuse of the poor:

> They occupy seats of power
> And mete out injustice to the poor

They write inventories of the pantry
Thinking of ghee, oil, and soap
They become the hired servants of the corrupt...[19]

Writing with a sense of indignation, Tukaram expressed what most peasants experienced in their daily lives: more powerful figures taking advantage of their positions to exploit the poor. Ambar's effective administration, land revenue reforms, religious tolerance, and respect for civil and criminal justice were viewed as a counterweight to the endemic forms of corruption and opportunism that ruined lives and corroded society. For this, Ambar was both praised and remembered.

CHAPTER 8

| JUSTICE, LAND REFORM, |
AND LEGACY

TRAVELING FROM THE PORT OF Surat to the Nizam Shahi in 1615, Pieter Gillis van Ravesteyn, a Gujarati-based Dutch factor, had a chance to meet Malik Ambar. Impressed by the distinguished Regent of Ahmednagar, the Dutchman described the military leader, administrator, and statesman as a "well-built man of life *and* suffering" [emphasis added]. He also noted that Ambar was "of more than normal height [and as] dark as a blackmoor." More pertinent to his trade mission, however, was Gillis van Ravesteyn's observation that "Excellent justice was maintained in [Ambar's regime] and was honored by everyone."[1] Having justice honored bode well for trade.

Two years later, affirming Gillis Van Ravesteyn's observations, another Dutchman of the Dutch East India Company, the officer Pieter van den Broecke, noted "Melick keeps good order and laws in his country, punishes criminals and thieves severely, and one can travel with gold through his land without any uneasiness." But Ambar's rules and the justice he practiced could also be harsh: "When somebody gets drunk," Van den Broecke continues, "[the Regent] has molten lead poured into his throat; nobody is allowed to sell liquor, or even travel with it through the country." More a practical matter than a religious mandate (Muslims are not supposed to drink alcohol), by punishing drunkenness Ambar would help keep the realm in order. Such "order and laws" made it possible for people to travel across the sultanate without fear, as Van den Broecke notes, and as alluded to by his compatriot two years earlier, promoted greater flow of trade, wealth, and monies for the use of the defense of the Nizam Shahi.[2]

It was perhaps a combination of fear and respect that resulted in what various observers described as Ambar's "popularity": Justice equally applied, even if harsh, led to more security and greater prosperity. While Ambar had his detractors, his mostly even-handed justice, practice of religious tolerance, and land revenue reform (on balance, positive for both peasants *and* the state treasury) gained him widespread support and admiration. As a result, Ambar received high praise from his contemporaries in India. Fuzuni Astarabadi writes that Ambar dealt even-handed justice to his people, keeping both his soldiers and farmers content; meanwhile, Muhammed Qasim Ferishta described Ambar as "the first general, politician and financier of his age, and his country was best cultivated, and his subjects the happiest of any in [the] Deccan . . . His charities and justice are yet celebrated; and he was also eminent for his piety."[3]

Ambar's piety likely shaped his sense of justice; or, perhaps, his sense of justice was expressed *as* piety, among other ways. To be sure, the Qur'an provided Ambar with guidance in how he should rule: "For Allah loves those who do good" (Surah Ali 'Imran 3:134) and "Allah loves those who are fair (and just)" (Surah Al Hujurat 49:9).[4] But what was "good" or "fair" was often the subject of wide interpretation among Muslims, despite their shared religion. The Sultanate of Ahmednagar had a majority Hindu population with its own legal traditions; following the practice of earlier Muslim rulers, such as Akbar or the Nizam Shahs of the Deccan, Ambar's position was one of religious tolerance.

As Regent, Ambar made some executive orders, but most of the laws of the land were derived from existing customs and codes of conduct. While other rulers interfered in the execution of legal processes, giving or gaining favors as they so desired, Ambar chose not to interfere with the courts. Instead, he allowed them to carry out their work whenever and wherever government machinery was in place to do so. Most cases were decided through the *Gotsabha*, a body of kinsmen, or, to a lesser extent, the *Des'aksabha*, a group of local leaders that included landholders. Very few cases were decided through the distinctly Hindu *Brahaman-Sabha*; finally, and only on occasion, cases were taken up by the *Raj-Sabha*, in which the sultan and his officers participated. The *Gotsabha* was perhaps the most commonly used process since it was inexpensive and quick. It mostly covered cases dealing with property disputes and some minor criminal offenses; more serious offenses were litigated by higher bodies with the presence of outside officials. The next level, *Des'aksabha*, could include the presence of a government official or the local *qadi* (a judge trained in Islamic law). For those who chose to enter into the *Brahaman-Sabha* process, notably *including* Muslim litigants, a body of learned Brahmins (upper-caste Hindus) would adjudicate in accordance with Hindu law. A feature of this customary form of law would include the ancient practice of ordeal, a tradition found among societies across the world (from Europe and Africa to other parts of Asia). In the Deccan it was called *Rava*, in which one's guilt or innocence was determined by one's survival (or degree of scathing) in "picking an ironball out of boiled oil."[5]

Taxes largely derived from land revenue ultimately affected more people than individual legal rulings in terms of the general population, of which the vast majority were land-cultivating peasants. Land-derived taxes were based on crop yield and paid for the army and maintenance of the sultanate's forts. Ambar drew approximately one quarter of cultivators' yields. His land revenue reform consisted of *nazar pahani*, the surveying (by "glance") of all lands based on a measurement (*bigha*) that assessed the *potential for crop yield*, not the area of land per se. Under this system a cultivator with twice as much land could be responsible for the same amount in taxes as someone with half the amount of land if the former's property was deemed less fertile (e.g., hilly tracts). In this way, taxes were settled on "a rational basis so that the collectors of the government might not oppress or harass the peasantry." The system, built on the pioneering work of Emperor Akbar's Revenue Minister, Todar Mal, allowed the people to have "a sense of security to reap the fruit of their hard and strenuous labour." Under Ambar's land revenue reform, peasants therefore paid what they could actually bear and had an incentive for greater productivity. As Tamaskar notes, the system "proved of immense benefit both to the state and the peasantry of the kingdom, as it offered stimulus [for] increased farming activities."[6]

Land revenue was supplemented by taxes on industries, including cotton and silk textiles at Bhiwandi, as well as woodworking and shipbuilding at Chaul. Additionally, there were the traditional industries that Ambar encouraged, including iron smelting, metalworking, and the manufacture of earthenware, glass, jewelry, and footwear. Taxes were levied logically on items for purchase with the long-term view of promoting greater production and income for the state. Land revenue permitted a number of other functions, from the upkeep of palaces and other governmental structures to the issuing of grants to Hindus and the building of mosques for Muslims. In the midst of political pressures and military imperatives, Ambar patronized the arts, music, and public building projects, becoming, as one scholar put it, "the nucleus of the revival of the cultural traditions of Ahmednagar."[7] For Ambar this culminated in his vision of a model city: Khirki.

Located on the Kham River in the valley of Dudhana between the Sathara mountain range and the Lakenvara hills northeast of Ahmednagar, Khirki sits at a crossroads of the region's major trade routes. As Ferishta writes, "[Ambar] founded [the city and] ornamented it with a magnificent palace, gardens, and noble pieces of water lined with stone."[8] In a number of ways

Khirki was Ambar's hope and view of the sultanate's future. During his first decade of rule, Ambar had moved the Nizam Shahi capital several times—from Parenda to Junnar, from Junnar to Daulatabad, and then finally to Khirki. Ambar shifted his capital to Khirki in 1612 after fending off another Mughal campaign against him. The new city, which was built on an older, smaller settlement, was closer to the Mughal frontier and in a well-sheltered geographical spot guarding a critical passage from the northwest to the east.[9]

Having settled in Khirki after a string of military victories between 1605 and 1612, Ambar signed a peace treaty with the Mughals that was upheld for two years. It was during this time that he began introducing far-reaching reforms in land revenue and military administration. But in February 1616 Khirki was attacked and plundered by the Mughals. As the Bijapuri court chronicler Fuzuni Astarabadi recounts,

> [Mughal General] Shah Nawaz Khan burnt and totally desolated the country from Paitan to Khirki. The houses of Ambar were not allowed to be ravaged, but in the city of Khirki the devastation went beyond all limits. Ambar took refuge in Daulatabad fort. Peace was now made on condition of the Deccani Sultans paying 12 lakhs of *hun* to the prince, the nobles, and Shah Nawaz Khan. [It was only at that point that the] Mughal generals returned to their stations.[10]

Ambar was determined to rebuild Khirki, and did so with vigor and spirit. But, once again, the Mughals attacked and destroyed the city. This time, in 1621, the Mughal Prince Khurram—the future Emperor Shah Jahan—led the destruction. Undeterred, Ambar and his city, like the phoenix of Herodotus' Greece or the Garuda bird of Hindu legend, rose again. But Khirki was sapped of its vitality, much like Baghdad, whose splendor had been significantly lost after Mongol destruction three centuries earlier but still served as a model of cosmopolitan life for Ambar. Still,

Khirki remained a symbol of urban sophistication built around rational planning, design, and construction. The underground waterworks of Khirki, reminiscent of the Persian qanat system, provided water to much of the city and long remained evidence of Ambar's precise and visionary engineering. Another illuminating feature of the city—its division of quarters—included the subdivisions of Malpura, Khelpura, and Vithapura, which Ambar named in honor of his great Hindu Maratha chiefs.

Ambar's trusted right-hand man Maloji Raje Bhosale, and his son, Shahaji Raje Bhosale, had both led Maratha forces that made up Ambar's formidable army. Here Muslims and Marathas had united to resist Mughal hegemony in their shared bid to preserve their distinct political and regional identity. Just as Ambar expressed his gratitude toward the Marathi people by naming the districts of his beloved city after some of their leaders, the Marathas of Maharashta expressed their gratitude to Ambar in their oral tradition. Among the stories that would emerge in the Deccan is a tale appearing in *Tarikh-i-Shivaji* about Ambar's rise to power. As the historian Jagindra Nath Chowdhuri recounts,

> It is stated . . . that [Ambar] came from Bijapur to Daulatabad as a dervish [ascetic], and while he was sleeping in a shop on the roadside with his legs raised, Sabaji Anant, an influential [Maratha] Nizam Shahi nobleman, happened to pass by that road in a palanquin. His eyes fell upon the soles of the feet of Malik Ambar and he discerned in them the marks of fortune. It was evident to him that this man was "either a chieftain, or a chieftain's son. He awakened him," "took him to his house," and, after performing all the formalities made him the naib of the kingdom with due pomp and grandeur.[11]

Although apocryphal, the story was likely invented as a way of honoring Ambar but perhaps also to claim his success as having been foretold, if not facilitated, by a Maratha. In certain respects, Ambar's military success was in fact due to the Maratha; without their light cavalry force, Ambar would not have been able to defend the Deccan for so long.

Ambar lived a long and extraordinary life. Mughal and Bijapuri court chroniclers describe news of his passing away and of his accomplishments. Mu'tamad Khan, the author of the *Tuzuk-i Jahangiri*, writes:

> Intelligence now arrived of the death of Ambar the Abyssinian, in the 80th year of his age, on 31st *Urdibihist* [May 14, 1626]. This Ambar was a slave, but an able man. In warfare, in command, in sound judgement, and in administration, he had no rival or equal. He well understood that predatory (*kazzaki*) warfare, which in the language of the Dakhin is called *bari-giri*. He kept down the turbulent spirits of that country, and maintained his exalted position to the end of his life, and closed his career in honour. History records no other instance of an Abyssinian slave arriving at such eminence.[12]

The Bijapuri court chronicler Ferishta writes:

> Ambar has leisure to regulate his country, levy great armies and even dared to seize some of the imperial districts. When the authority of Jahangir was established, he sent frequent armies to the Deccan; but Ambar was not to be subdued, and, though sometimes defeated, continued to oppose the royal strength . . . [He] conducted his affairs with much glory, after obliging the Sultans of Golkunda and Bijapur to pay him contributions. He died in the year 1035 [A.H.] in this eighteenth year and was buried . . . under a splendid dome which he had erected.[13]

In the village of Ambarpur, near Khultabad, stands Malik Ambar's tomb (*dargah*), which he helped to design and build.[14] Notably, the tomb, which is made of a dark reddish basalt, closely follows the plan of Chand Bibi's at Gulbarga to the southeast. Standing right next to Ambar's tomb, however, is that of his wife,

Bibi Karima.[15] The architectural historian Klaus Rotzer describes the tomb in these terms: "The mosque and portico . . . open outwards, so that it may be used by the public. Here may be seen the desire to see to the people's well-being, which was a central feature of Malik Ambar's character." He continues,

> Its technical perfection and the high quality of the materials with which it was built were more important than its visual effect. The tomb was built to last . . . Compared to the neighbouring tombs it seems to be a synthesis of what was being done at the time of this construction, and a model for the future architecture of the Ahmednagar sultanate. It was intended to be the expression of a united Deccani society. By their Muslim form, the *samadhis* [shrines] at Ellora show that the Hindu Bhonsles shared this vision.[16]

Today, the *muezzin*'s call may still be heard faintly in and around Ambar's *dargah* in the early mornings and evenings—the same prayer call heard during the height of Ambar's rule. Nearly

Tomb (dargah) *of Malik Ambar designed by Malik Ambar, Khuldabad, India.*

three centuries ago the Governor of Berar, Nawab Shahnawaz Khan, included the Abyssinian Regent in a biographical dictionary of prominent Deccani figures. Although Khan passed away before completing the book, his son Abdul Hai Khan finished the task. Noting that Ambar protected the poor, the biographical entry places the Abyssinian within the larger context of the African diaspora in the Indian Ocean world:

> [Ambar] laboured much in protecting the peasantry and in the advancement of agriculture. In spite of all the commotion and turmoil, for the Moghuls and the Deccanis were always fighting, he developed the village of Khirki, five *kos* from Daulatabad ... and made tanks, gardens and lofty buildings there. They say that in the distribution of charity and other good works, and in the administration of justice and the relief of the oppressed, he was very strong. He patronized poets. A certain poet has said in praise of him— There was Bilal, the servant of the Apostle of Allah; After one thousand years there came Malik Ambar.[17]

Khuldabad, located in the "valley of saints," would contain the tombs of several Muslim *pirs* (saints) whose charitable acts were renowned—including those of the Chishti Order (followers of Moinuddin Chishti, the thirteenth-century Afghani-born Sufi known as the "Benefactor of the Poor").[18] There are multiple accounts regarding Ambar's own charity. Mughal, Bijapuri, and Europeans all note his actions toward the poor. For instance, the Englishman William Minor described how a "galliot [a type of ship] of Chaule was the Mallacambars [*sic*] and has brought rice for the poor, which he yearly sends."[19]

As the historian Richard Eaton notes, Ambar's career provides "a window onto a range [of] issues pertaining to the social history of the Deccan—issues of race, class, or gender, and especially issues related to the institution of slavery."[20] While Ambar may have retained certain memories or nostalgia about his childhood and family in Ethiopia, he may have also tried to eviscerate

memories too painful to want to recall. He seems to have maintained a connection with fellow Abyssinians through his marriage to Bibi Karima, a Siddi, and the appointment of several
Abyssinians to high posts, such as Siddi Yakub Khan, who apparently won his confidence. But he also locked horns with several
African *amirs*, most notably Ikhlas Khan. Ultimately, several of
his Abyssinian confidants left the Nizam Shahi to join either the
Adil Shahi or the Mughals. Regarding his cavalry force Commander-in-Chief Siddi Yakub Khan, one contemporary Indian
source notes:

> Intelligence arrived from the Dakhin that Yakub Khan, the Abys-
> sinian, who, in that country, was next in rank to Malik 'Ambar, and
> during his life even had held important commands, had now deter-
> mined to make his submission to the Imperial throne. Khan Jahan
> wrote to Yakub in warm and assuring terms, and directed the
> *amirs* to receive him with all hospitality and respect, and to bring
> him to Burhanpur.[21]

Lower-ranking Abyssinians also left Ambar. In about 1610,
Malik Sandal, an African eunuch, opposed Ambar's rule and left
for Bijapur.[22] But Ambar retained his own fidelity to salt; for him
it was to Chengiz Khan, whom Ambar honored by naming his
second son after him and by presenting himself as the deceased
Abyssinian *peshwa*'s slave nearly fifty years after his former master's death. As Rotzer notes, "an inscription over the east gate of
Dagar Ghoddi at Junnar describes him as 'Chengiz Khani,' meaning that Malik Ambar was a slave of Chengiz Khan and continued
to style himself so after the death of his master and after he was a
great and powerful figure in his own right."[23]

There are questions about his relationship and the importance of his wife. In the "taking" of a wife, which is the way his
marriage is noted, akin to a purchase or transaction, it is never
considered that his wife may have been a source of political
advice. The fact that she was his only wife, and buried next to

him, may signify something more to their relationship. To what, if any, extent did she play in his decisions as a confidante and advisor? For instance, did she help or guide him in his decision to marry off their daughter to the Nizam Shah? She was likely another source of support and wisdom in his ability to survive, and for so long. To be sure, Ambar was a rebel but not a revolutionary: He largely maintained the socioeconomic structure of the Deccan. It may very well be that Ambar lasted as long as he did because he remained within the accepted social and cultural boundaries of his time and place. His administration was inclusive, based not on religion or race but on loyalty, ability, and effectiveness.[24]

Ambar may have been patient, but in all things he did not wait for circumstances to unfold. Like a master chess player (the word "chess" is derived from the Persian and Urdu word for "king," "shah") he thought in multiple moves. As a strategic matter, Ambar never assumed a formal position greater than regent or prime minister. By retaining the traditional court structure, or the appearance thereof, he maintained a degree of legitimacy, pre-empting accusations of usurping the throne. Ambar's military and political career in Ahmednagar and Bijapur would span over fifty years. It was equivalent to that of Emperor Akbar, who was six years his elder, but whom Ambar outlived by over two decades.

At some point in his old age Ambar would have likely felt the need to acknowledge that, one day, he too would pass away, if not by murder then by natural causes. His doing so may have freed him to think more deeply about his own mortality and perhaps the ways in which he may have erred as a Muslim in pursuing his defense of the Deccan. Looking back, Ambar had certainly come a long distance from the days of his Oromo youth in Abyssinia. He had transformed himself from an enslaved subject of several masters across the Indian Ocean world into a kingmaker and ruler of the Deccan. He had faithfully toiled to preserve the Sultanate of Ahmednagar and to uphold the idea of a Nizam Shahi. Would he have been satisfied with what he accomplished?

We end with Ambar's own words. During a much earlier time, soon after the turn of the seventeenth century when the Mughals had taken over Ahmednagar, Ambar asked the Adil Shah if he would return to the kingdom the Fort of Qandahar, which had long been part of the Nizam Shahi but had fallen into the hands of Bijapur in 1600:

> It is my design to fight the Mughal troops so long as life remains in this body. It may be that through your Majesty's daily increasing fortune I shall expel the Mughals from the Deccan. But I have no place where I can leave my children with composure of mind before engaging the enemy. It would not be far from your royal grace to grant me the fort of Qandahar, which your officers have captured again after the olden times.[25]

Here we catch a glimpse of Ambar, the diplomat and the father. As a diplomat he sought peace where war could be avoided; as a father he sought his children's security and welfare. Astarabadi describes what happened next: "[The] Adil Shah granted [his] prayer, and gave him that fort. When Ambar took possession of Qandahar, a new splendor and strength was gained by him, and his power daily increased."[26]

Over the years Ambar's "splendor and strength" grew with his patience and pragmatism. Time and again his foresight and flexibility allowed him to successfully defend not only the Nizam Shahi but the Deccan as a whole. In that protracted struggle—in that long journey—a world away from his original homeland, Ambar ruled justly, created family, renewed a sultanate, and improved the lives of the poor. Just as importantly, for over two and a half decades he kept the Mughals at bay.

| ABYSSINIAN DEFENDER | OF THE DECCAN

THE MUGHAL EMPEROR JAHANGIR, WHO died just one year after Malik Ambar passed away, may have been pleased to hear the news that his nemesis was finally gone. Ambar's eldest son Fateh Khan, who took over as Regent, however, would deny the emperor the pleasure of conquering the Nizam Shahi. Under the weight of the Mughal armies and their Deccani allies, Khan was only able to hold out for so long. In 1633 Ambar's son was forced to hand over the young Sultan of Ahmednagar, Hussain Nizam Shah, to the Mughals. He did so along with other members of the royal family, ending nearly 150 years of dynastic rule. But then came a sudden turn of events.

The Maratha commander Shahaji Raje Bhonsle, who had fought with Ambar in the Battle of Bhatvadi but had since gone into the service of Bijapur, installed a new boy sultan as Murtaza Nizam Shah III with the help of the Adil Shah (the Nizam Shahi's off-again, now on-again ally), breathing new life into Ahmednagar, just as Ambar had done over three decades earlier. But like Fateh Khan, Shahaji could not withstand the imperialist forces, holding out for just three more years—that is, until 1636. In that year the Mughals under Prince Aurangzeb led imperial armies at his father Emperor Shah Jahan's direction, wresting control of the rebel sultanate and absorbing it into the empire. What neither

107

Akbar nor Jahangir was able to do, Aurangzeb accomplished for his father, Shah Jahan, who had rebelled against his father, just as his grandfather had rebelled against his. Without a clear line of succession (for instance, with the system of primogeniture, where the eldest son assumes the throne upon the king's death), brother fought brother. In Aurangzeb's case, he would imprison his father *and* kill his brother, Dara Shikoh, in order to become emperor.

In the end, Ambar's model city, Khirki, twice destroyed by the Mughals during his lifetime, was renamed Aurangabad, in honor of the emperor Aurangzeb (whose piety took him down a very different path than the one Ambar created).[1] Within a generation after the end of the Nizam Shahi, both Bijapur and Golconda would also fall under the weight of the imperial Mughal armies. And yet the seeds of resistance had already been sown in a line of extraordinary warriors Ambar had helped to inspire and train: the Maratha warriors of the Bhonsle clan, as seen most spectacularly in the career of the Deccan's next and most outstanding rebel leader, Shivaji Bhonsle—Maloji Raje Bhonsle's grandson and Shahaji's son (the latter two having served in Ambar's army at high ranks). Born in the city of Junnar located in the district of Puna, Shivaji would effectively press the Mughals back. Perhaps as a child hearing stories of the Regent of Ahmednagar at the Battle of Bhatvadi, where his father led Maratha troops under Ambar's general command, he caught the spirit of rebellion passed down from one generation to the next: Chand Bibi to Ambar, Ambar to Shahaji, and finally Shahaji to Shivaji. In creating a counterweight to Mughal imperialism, Shivaji drew upon some of the same organizing and guerrilla tactics used by those who preceded him, most effectively developed and practiced by the Abyssinian defender of the Deccan—Malik Ambar.[2]

TIMELINE

1530s—Start of Oromo migration from southern to central Ethiopia.

1540s—Ethiopian Christians and Muslim Adal Sultanate at war.

1548—Malik Ambar (Chapu) born in Hararghe, Ethiopia.

1551–1568—Oromo and Amirate of Harar are at war.

circa 1560—Ambar is captured, taken to Mocha, and purchased by Kazi Hussein.

circa 1565—Taken to Baghdad, purchased by the chief *qadi* of Mecca, Qazi-ul-Quzat, and then resold and educated by Mir Qasim.

1565–1588—Reign of Murtaza Nizam Shah I; Regency of the pro-Afaqi (new settlers) Queen Hadia; in 1569 Hadia is overthrown by the Deccanis, who included the Abyssinian Habash Khan.

circa 1571—Ambar arrives in Deccan; purchased by Mirak Dabir (Chengiz Khan), *peshwa* (prime minister) of the Nizam Shahi.

1569–1574—Dominance of Chengiz Khan in the court of the Ahmednagar Sultanate, Murtaza Nizam Shah I; Khan is murdered in 1574.

1573—Gujarat, to the north of Ahmednagar, is annexed by the Mughals, end of Gujarati Sultanate.

1575–1595—Ambar serves as a mercenary and midlevel commander in Bijapur; Chand Bibi is Regent of Bijapur from 1580 to 1590.

1594—Portuguese try to avoid open conflict with Ambar.

1595—Death of Ibrahim Nizam Shahi; Chand Bibi begins as Regent of Ahmednagar; Mughals launch attack on Fort of Ahmednagar, which is repelled by Bibi; Ambar breaks through Mughal lines under Abhang Khan's command but is unable to defeat the superior forces; goes into countryside and wages attacks from there.

1596—Ambar gathering forces in the countryside and serves as petty chief of Chaul and Dabul; Abhang Khan serves as Bibi's *peshwa*.

1600 CE/1009 AH—Mughals capture Fort of Ahmednagar in August; Ambar installs Murtaza Nizam Shah II and becomes *de facto* ruler of the sultanate of Ahmednagar, serving as *peshwa* and Regent; he has his daughter married to the young sultan; founding of the British East India Company.

1601—Ambar wounded at Nandere and saved by his soldiers; the Portuguese fear an attack on Goa by Ambar; Ambar makes a truce with the Mughals in December.

1602—Ambar wounded again and barely escapes, this time at Qandahar; Ambar marches against Bidar in March; the Dutch East India Company is founded; Mughal court chronicler Abu'l-Fazl ibn Mubarak, author of the *Akbarnama*, is murdered by Prince Salim (soon Emperor Jahangir) because of his opposition to the prince's accession to the throne.

1604—Ambar defends Nizam Shahi against a Mughal attack.

1605 CE/1014 AH—Death of Mughal Emperor Akbar; his son Jahangir assumes the throne; Portuguese authorities in India are urged by Philip II to induce Ambar to oppose Mughals.

1607—Deccani rival Miyan Raju is imprisoned by Ambar after capturing Daulatabad and Junnar; Jahangir sends armies to destroy Ambar.

1609 CE/1018 AH—Fateh Khan, Ambar's son, marries daughter of Yaqut Khan, a Habshi and one of Bijapur's leading nobleman; Ambar launches an attack on an English caravan.

1610 CE/1019 AH—Ambar recaptures Ahmednagar in May and transfers the capital from Junnar to Daulatabad; Ambar has his son-in-law Murtaza Nizam Shah II poisoned along with his senior Persian wife, and installs the deceased sultan's son as Burham Nizam Shah III (who rules until 1631); Ambar builds the city of Khirki (Fatehnagar, "city of victory").

1612—After unbroken victories between 1605 and 1612 Ambar signs a peace treaty with Mughals, which is upheld for two years; Ambar introduces far-reaching reforms in revenue and military administration; Muhammed Qasim Ferishta completes his *Tarikh-i-Ferishta*.

1613—Ambar and Mughals attack Portuguese possessions; assassination attempt by Rajputs on Ambar.

1614—Rebellion of Nizam Shahi chiefs against Ambar; siege of Chaul, Daman, and Bassein in November.

1615—Tripartite treaty among the Portuguese, Malik Ambar, and Adil Shah against the Mughals.

1616—Khirki plundered and destroyed by Mughals in February, but rebuilt; Abu'l-Hasan paints Jahangir's fantasy shooting of Ambar.

1617—Ambar loses Ahmednagar to Mughals in June; Ambar meets with the Dutch merchant Pieter van den Broecke.

1618—Adil Shah quarrels with Ambar around midyear.

1619—Ambar and his allies invade Mughal territory in May.

1620—Ambar and his allies near Mebkar, accompanied by Maloji, grandfather of Shivaji Bhosale; Mirza Asad Beg notes Ambar's numerous qualities.

1621—Khirki once again destroyed, this time by Shah Jahan, Mughal prince; efforts by Ibrahim Adil Shah II agent to assassinate Ambar in October; capture of Ambar's frigates on September 29 by the English.

1622—Rebellion by Shah Jahan against Emperor, attempt to ally with Ambar.

1624 CE/1033 AH—Battle of Bhatvadi against combined forces of the Mughals and Bijapur and with support of Golconda; Maratha Shahaji Raje Bhosale leads forces.

1626 CE/1035 AH—Ambar dies in Khirki on May 11 of natural causes and is buried at his tomb in Ambarpur, near Khuldabad; his son, Fateh Khan, begins serving as *peshwa* of the Nizam Shahi.

1627—Emperor Jahangir dies; Mughal court chronicler Mu'tamad Khan completes *Iqbal-nama-yi Jahangiri*.

1631—Mughals capture Dharur; its commander, Sidi Salim Habashi, surrenders.

1632—Mughal envoy Mirza Asad Beg comments in his memoirs about Ambar's charity in approximately 1620.

1633—Shah Jahan captures Daulatabad; beginning of Murtaza Nizam Shah III's reign; after a falling out with Fateh Khan, Murtaza comes under the dominance of the Abyssinian Hamid Khan and his wife.

1636—Fateh Khan murders Murtaza Nizam Shah III and replaces him with the latter's son as a puppet ruler; Shah Jahan annexes the Ahmednagar Sultanate; Fateh Khan and Hamid Khan are given pensions.

1643—The Adil Shah court chronicler Fuzuni Astarabadi completes his *Fatuhat-i-Adil Shah*.

1674—Shivaji Bhosale, the grandson of Ambar's commander Maloji Raje Bhosale, leads Marathas in the creation of the Maratha Confederacy.

PRIMARY SOURCE EXCERPTS AND STUDY QUESTIONS

THE BOOK HAS EXPLORED THE interrelated themes of power and slavery across the Indian Ocean. In particular it has looked at (1) the possibilities for upward mobility of enslaved Africans through the institution of military slavery and (2) the political and diplomatic struggles of imperial powers with smaller polities. As you examine the following excerpts from a number of different primary sources, consider these themes.

I.
KING PHILIP II, 1596, 1601, 1604

King Philip II of Spain (and Portugal) was keenly interested in Ambar, whom he sought as an ally against the Mughals. In a series of letters to his viceroys Dom Francisco de Gama and Ayres de Saldana, he discusses his strategic thinking regarding Ambar:

Matias de Albuqurque [the former viceroy] wrote me also that his embassy to the Idalcao [Adilkhan] [the king of Bijapur] was intended to make an alliance with the Mellique [the petty chief of Chaul and Dabul] in order to be ready against the Moghul [emperor]; and to attain better this object, he mentioned to him many reasons showing him the evident danger for these kings of

Note: There are several variations of the name Malik Ambar that are used in the document, including Melick and Mellick.

ruining themselves altogether, should they not ally and strengthen themselves against the Moghuls; to this you must help also persuading all those kings one after another, a task that will become easier with the Mellique [Malik] at present, since peace has already being settled [with him], according to the news of Matias de Albuquerque that came by land.[1]

And though the Conde [de Vidiguera] writes me that Akbar is already an old man, distrusting his eldest son and fearing to be poisoned by him and (on account that) he had stopped the war he was waging against the kingdom of Mellique [Malik], yet since that king is very powerful and sagacious and desirous of approaching to the island of Goa, I recommend you to keep your eyes open on his designs and design to prevent them with the necessary remedies.[2]

The circumstances of the relations between Akbar and his eldest son, as related by you, are the most suitable for the welfare of that State; and since we know the purpose of that kind, I wish that the discord between them would last until his death, for after his demise it is understood that war will ensue in all his kingdom. The precautions taken by the Mellique [Malik], to defend himself from him, as you told me, must be much appreciated, and I thank you for the pains you are taking to induce and incite him to do so.[3]

II.
ABU'L-FAZL IBN MUBARAK, 1602

Abu'l-Fazl ibn Mubarak, the Mughal court chronicler of Emperor Akbar, was the principal author of the Akbarnama

---

1. Philip II to Viceroy Dom Francisco de Gama, February 25, 1596; *Livros das Monções de Reino*, No. 4, Ano de 1595 to 1598, fol. 629, Goa Historical Archives.
2. Philip II to Viceroy Ayres de Sadana, January 25, 1601; *Livros das Monções do Reino*, No. 8, Ano de 1601 to 1602, fol. 18, Goa Historical Archives.
3. Philip II to Viceroy Ayres de Sadana, March 23, 1604; *Livros das Monções do Reino*, No. 9, Ano de 1604, fol. 22, Goa Historical Archives.

("Book of Akbar"). Here he describes the Mughal armies'
battles with Ambar's forces:

Good men went to that country [Deccan] and defeated the enemy,
and praiseworthy efforts were made to keep that country in repose.
One of the occurrences was the victory of Īrīj, the son of the Khān-
khānān and the defeat of 'Ambar Jeo [Malik Ambar]. News came
that when it was known that 'Ambar had gone to Telingāna and
that Mīr Martaẓā had not been able to maintain himself in Nānder,
and that he and Sher Khwāja had gone to the village of Jahrī, and
that the enemy was being powerful in that country, and that Sher
Khwaja and Mīr Martaẓā were in distress, the Khān-khānān had
sent his son Irij with a large force to quell the commotion. Irij
joined Mīr Martaẓā and Sher Khwaja, and resolved to engage the
enemy. On learning this, 'Ambar went to Damtour and from there
proceeded to Qandahar. Meanwhile Farhad Abyssinian joined
'Ambar with 2 or 3,000 horses. The brave men of the victorious
army did not halt anywhere but advanced towards the foe. As
the enemy stood their ground, the leaders of the victorious army
drew up their forces. In the centre was Irij and his father's troops
and *mansabdhars*. In the advance were … S. Mastafa, Fath K. Lodi,
Ikhtiyar K., Sher K. and other heroes. In the right wing were
Mīr Martaẓā and a number of active men. In the left wing were 'Ali
Mardan Bahadur, and a party of brave men. 'Ambar also drew up
his forces. First, the enemy's van drove off the elephants and attacked the imperial van, and there was a hot fight. From the smoke
of the guns and muskets day put on the dark robes of night. The
brave imperialists discomfited the foe by their bullets and the
whizzing of their arrows. Then the centre made manful attacks. . . .
If the men of the right and left wings had extended the arm of courage, the enemy would not have escaped, and 'Ambar and Farhād
would certainly have been made prisoners. Twenty elephants
[among other possessions] were captured. When the news of this
glorious victory was brought to His Majesty by a report of Prince

Daniel, thanks were returned to God. The victors were rewarded by promotion and gifts of horses and robes of honour. The Prince sent ten of the elephants to court, and kept ten by himself, with the idea that he would present them whenever he came to court . . .[4]

III.
MUHAMMED QASIM FERISHTA, 1612

Muhammed Qasim Ferishta, a Persian historian who served as the captain of the guards of Murtaza Nizam Shah in Ahmednagar before moving into the service of Ibrahim Adil Shah II of Bijapur, completed his Tarikh-i Firishta in 1612. It was translated by the East India Company officer General John Briggs in eight volumes as The History of the Rise of the Mahometan Power in India. Ferishta offers some of the most detailed descriptions of the diplomatic and military actions taken by Malik Ambar.

[At Nandere] a severe action took place, in which many soldiers were slain on both sides, and the Deccanis were eventually defeated. Mullick Ambur, who lay wounded on the field, was only saved by the devoted gallantry of his attendants from falling a prisoner into the enemy's hands; an object they effected after losing a number of men. Mullick Ambur no sooner recovered from his wounds than he began to collect more troops; Khan Khanan, well aware of his enterprising character and popularity in the country, feared the Moghuls might be eventually overpowered by numbers under so active a leader, and for these reasons made overtures for peace: while Mullick Ambur, on the other hand, aware of the enmity of Meean Rajoo, and not without suspicions even of his having urged the late attack, gladly accepted the offer,

---

4. Abu'l-Fazl ibn Mubarak, *The Akbarnama of Abu-l-Fazl*, Vol. 3, Henry Beveridge, trans. (Calcutta: Asiatic Society of Bengal, 1909), 1211-1212.

and a treaty was concluded which marked out their respective future boundaries . . . At this period . . . Furhad Khan . . . and Mullick Sundul, an eunuch, with other officers, deserted Mullick Ambur, and joined Murtaza Nizam Shah II at Owsa, where they collected a force. Mullick Ambur, marching against this faction, dispersed it . . . As Mullick Ambur had long wished to obtain possession of Purenda, he took the king to that fortress; the governor of which Mittun Khan, an Abyssinian, who had been nearly twenty years in the situation, intimated to the King that he was willing to receive and admit him as his liege lord; but that Mullick Ambur, having made peace with the Mogul general, had in fact become one of that party, and he therefore refused to receive him within the walls. Mullick Ambur replied, that it was true that he had been compelled, on account of the late conspiracy against him, to be on friendly terms with Khan Khanan, but that he was a true and loyal servant of the Nizam Shah family, and was ready to support it with his last breath. The governor was not moved by these arguments; and Mullick Ambur, to prevent the King uniting with Mittun Khan, kept him for the present a state prisoner. The moment that Furhad Khan and Mullick Sundul heard of the King's confinement, they flew to Purenda, and threw themselves into the fort, which was defended for upwards of a month against Mullick Ambur; but the governor's son having committed some cruelty on the inhabitants of the place, they rebelled and slew him, and his father was himself compelled to fly, accompanied by Furhad Khan and Mullick Sundul, to Beejapoor, where they entered into the service of the Adil Shahy monarch. The garrison of Purenda held out for some time longer, till at length Mullick Ambur having re-moved all restraint from Moortaza Nizam Shah II, he was permit-ted to introduce the King into it, while himself remained encamped without . . .

In the year 1016 [1607 c.e.] . . . Murtaza Nizam Shah II, accom-panied by his general, Mullick Ambur, marched at the head of ten thousand cavalry from Parenda against Junnar, which that monarch now again made the seat of the Nizam Shahy government, whence he despatched an army to Dowlu-tabad against Meean Rajoo. That chief, after a short time, was defeated and taken prisoner, and his country again reverted to Nizam Shahy authority. Mullick Ambur continues to add daily to his influence and power . . .[5]

IV.
PIETER VAN DEN BROECKE, 1617

The Dutch merchant Pieter van den Broecke met with Ambar in 1617. Van den Broecke, who became the manager of the Dutch East India Company, or VOC (Vereenigde Oostindische Compagnie), at Surat, notes how Ambar maintained law and order within the Nizam Shahi kingdom, and makes a number of other observations. On display is Ambar's diplomacy and regal command as he receives audience from an ambassador, hears from Portuguese renegades, and meets with the Dutch merchant himself.

In the afternoon I went in person to the Melick Ambahaer [Malik Ambar], bringing as presents a Japanese saber and an expensive Javanese kris. He liked the Japanese saber but not the kris, because it was decorated with a demon. He gave it back, gave me also a permit for the rest of our people, was very friendly, and hung two expensive *pomerins* [colored cloths] around my shoulders, one made of gold, the other one of camel's hair; this is the greatest honor one can give a person. He also offered to give me soldiers as a guard and convoy to Golconda.

He had with him an ambassador from King Partabasja [Partaba Shah?], who requested his horse back and compensations for damages done to his people. I told Mellick Ambaer that I was now in his land and under his authority; that I had come to his land trusting

5. Muhammed Qasim Ferishta (*Tarikh-i-Ferishta*), *History of the Rise of the Mohammedan Power in India*, Vol. III, John Briggs, trans. (New York: Cambridge University Press, 2013), 315–317, 320.

his word, since he is considered in the whole world as a man who scrupulously keeps his word. If it was his wish that I return the horse, then I would give it up, but not of my free will, indeed very much against it. But if this was not his wish, then the . . . soldiers should try to get it by force of arms. He began to laugh and gave the message to the ambassador, who did not like it a bit.

In our company were also some Portuguese *arnegados* [renegades] who said, in Portuguese, "Look at that proud dog," *Vede iste suberbe can!* They came to the Melick to request command of 3, 4, or 5,000 horses. They said: "This dog only comes to spy; watch out." With a friendly face he gave my leave and I rode back to my tent.

The Melick Ambar is a black kaffir from the land of Habessi [Abyssinia] or Preseter John's land. He has a stern Roman face, and is tall and strong of stature, with white glassy eyes which do not become him. He is a good administrator and was a slave who was sold for 20 ducats in Mocha. After the death of his master, who was a rich nobleman from the Deccan, he married the nobleman's widow, who did not have much property since the kings of those lands generally confiscate the property of the great lords. He therefore had to take to stealing and robbing, in which he was very successful, and attracted many followers, in the end even to the number of 5,000 horses. He began to dominate and with his robbers maintained himself against the king in an unassailable place where King Nisium Sia [Nizam Shah] could not harm him at all, because this fox was too smart for him; they were at war for many years. Then, because the king was also at war with the Great Mogul, who was trying to fish in this troubled water and become master of the Deccan, [the king] sent for Melick Ambahar and offered him an attractive income if he would return to his obedience and help him against the Great Mogul. The aforementioned Mellick, a cunning man, having noticed the guile and tricks of the king, refused and persisted in his plans, finally having over 8,000 mounted men. He became stronger and got more followers all the time. The king, seeing this, offered peace again. Mellick answered that he would be willing to serve against the Great Mogul and become the king's eternal vassal, on the condition that the king forgot about the past and agreed to marry Mellick's daughter as his queen. The king consented with approval of his council, married Mellick's daughter with great triumph and magnificence, and after that Mellick came with 8,000 well-equipped cavalry to court, where he was welcomed very much and given another 4,000 horses by the king, who thus placed him in direct command over 12,000 cavalry; he was held in high esteem by the king, who gave him considerable income.

At a certain time it happened that the king's wife, who was a white Persian woman, scolded the daughter of the aforementioned Melick Ambahaer with many bitter words, saying that she was only a kaffir woman and a concubine of the king and that her father had been a rebel against the king. The daughter informed her father of this through someone else, and her father then became so angry that he began to plot the murder of the king. He persuaded Mier Abdel Fatj [Amir 'Abd al-Fath], the king's secretary, to join him, and the latter poisoned the king a short time later with a potion. The king died immediately, leaving a young son whom Mellick Ambaer captured. He then proceeded to bring the whole country under his command.

The king's son is now already 12 years old; he was only 5 when his father died. The Mellick goes to greet him solemnly twice each week as a token of his obedience. The name of the young king is Nisiam Sia [Nizam Shah]. The queen who was the cause of this evil history was also poisoned, shortly after the king her husband.

The aforementioned Melick Ambahaar is now the Governor of the whole country, under the pretext that the king is too young. He carries on a vigorous war against the Great Mogul, and he is supported annually by the kings of Golconda, Visiapour [Bijapur], and Baligatte, to wit, by the king of Golconda, whose name is Cote Basja [Qutb Shah], with 6,000 men, by the king of Visiapour [Bijapur], Ebraham Sia [Ibrahim Shah], with 10,000 men, infantry as well as cavalry, by the king of Baligatte, near Goa, with 12,000 men, infantry and cavalry, plus some more from other little kings; this means that he has every year over 80,000 cavalry in his army, which he must keep continually together because of the Great Mogul, who often launches heavy attacks. If the Gatos [Ghats, mountain range] were not so dangerous to cross, he would have lost this land long ago, and that is the reason why they [Ambar's forces] must be constantly on their guard around this pass through the Gatos.

The aforementioned Melick keeps good order and laws in his country, punishes criminals and thieves severely, and one can travel with gold through his land without any uneasiness. When somebody gets drunk, he has molten lead poured into his throat; nobody is allowed to sell liquor, or even travel with it through the country. The army is very large ... At this time of the year it is very cold. In the army camp, called Kerka [Khirki—"rocky town," the fortress Ambar built near Dawlatabad], one can buy everything one can imagine.

The Mellick wanted very much to keep me in his service. He had an offer made to me of 100 pagodas per month and a nice *aldea* [village] or income from a village. There were many Portuguese in his service who had all converted to Islam; some had command over 1,000 horses, others over 3,000 and 5,000; one [was] called Mansour Gaen [Mansur Khan], a half-caste from India.[6]

V.
MIRZA ASAD BEG, 1620

The Mughal envoy Mirza Asad Beg describes in his personal memoirs, Waqiat-i-Asad Beg, Malik Ambar's religious practice:

This brave and discreet man, at the time when the Nawab Allabi [Abu'l-Fazl ibn Mubarak] was the *subhedar,* in great distraction came to him with a request for service in the army. But Raja Harbans,

6. With assistance from Daniel Prinz, the translation comes from W. Ph. Coolhaas, ed., *Pieter van den Broecke in Azië* (The Hague: Martinus Nijhoff, 1962), 1:146–151; see also Graham W. Irwin, *Africans Abroad: A Documentary History of the Black Diaspora in Asia, Latin America, and the Caribbean during the age of slavery* (New York: Columbia University Press, 1977), 152–155.

who was in charge of the affairs of the Deccanis, bore a grudge against him, and did not like him to be enrolled in the imperial service. He misrepresented him to the S'aikh, and Ambar had to go away in sheer disappointment. But the Almighty did not forsake him, and raised him to this noble rank and position. As this humble self had two or three times been considerate to him, it left a deep impression on him. Hence he also extended to this humble self a reception that surpassed the expectations of the world. Verily, if the virtues of this tree of Universe were to be set down even in part, it would require a chapter, nay an entire volume. One of his qualities was that in his camp every night twelve thousand men recite the Holy Quran. He offered his prayers with the common people whose number was never less than a thousand. His charities are beyond description.[7]

VI.
PIETRO DELLA VALLE, 1623

The Italian traveler Pietro della Valle recorded in 1623 the power and authority that Malik Ambar commanded in Ahmednagar, and both his talent for governing and commitment to the Nizam Shahi:

An Abyssinian slave of Moors Religion, called Malik Ambar, administers the state . . . with such authority, that at this day this territory is more generally known and called by the name of Malik's country than the Kingdom of Nizamschia. Nevertheless this Malik Ambar governs not fraudulently and with design to usurp, by keeping the King shut up, as I have sometime heard; but, according as I have better understood since from person informed nearer hand, he administers with great fidelity and

7. Mirza Asad Beg, *Waqiat-i-Asad Beg*, in Indian History Congress, Proceedings, 1941, 601–603; Bhaskar G. Tamaskar, *The Life and Work of Malik Ambar* (Delhi: Idarah-i Adabiyat-i Delli, 1978), 312, 323.

submission towards the young king whom they say, he hath provided or given to wife a daughter of his own, upon security that himself shall be the Governor of the whole state as long as he lives. This Malik Ambar is a man of great parts, and fit for Government, but, they say, very impious, addicted to sorcery, whereby it is through that he keeps himself in favour with his king, and that for works of Inchantments, (as to make prodigious buildings and with good luck, that the same may last perpetually and succeed well), he hath with certain superstitious uses in these countries committed most horrid impieties and cruelties, killing hundreds of his slaves' children and others, and offering them as sacrifice to the invoked devils, with other abominable stories which I have heard related; but, because not seen by myself, I affirm not for true.[8]

On October the one and thirtieth news came to Goa that Melik Ambar, who for a good while successfully warred against Adil Shah at length in a victory had taken one Mulla Muhammad, General of Adil Shah's army and much favored by him, who by his ill demeanor towards the said Melik (even so far as to endeavour to get him poisoned) was the occasion of the present war, wherein Melik's chief intent was to revenge himself on the said Mulla Muhammad, whom being thus taken, they say, he beheaded and caused him in that manner to be carried about his camp with this proclamation: that this traitor Mulla Muhammad, the cause of the war and present discords between Adil Shah and Nizam Shah (to whom this Melik is Governor) otherwise friends and allies, was thus in the name of his Lord Adil Shah, as a traitor and disturber of the public peace, put to death. By which act Melik meant to signify that he had no evil intention against Adil Shah but only took up Arms for the mischiefs done him by Mulla Muhammad, whom he desired to remove from the government . . . and from

8. Pietro della Valle; Sivaji Nibandhavali, II, 13; Bhaskar G. Tamaskar, *The Life and Work of Malik Ambar* (Delhi: Idarah-i Adabiyat-i Delli, 1978), 317.

the world. Yet it was not known how Adil Shah received this action, and what end the business would have.

In this war, they say, the Mughals favored Adil Shah against Melik and supplied him with 20,000 horses; but, be that how it will, Adil Shah hath hitherto always gone by the worst and some-times been in great danger; Melik, who is a brave Captain, having overrun all the State almost to the Gates of Bijapur, which is the Royal City of Adil Shah, where he has sometimes been forced to shut himself up as if it were besieged. A few months before, Adil Shah put one of his principal wives to death for conspiracy which she was said to hold with Melik, and for having been a party in promoting this war, out of design to [remove] Adil Shah from the Government, as one [who became] odious to his own people, either through his covetousness, or inability [being infirm], and to place his Son in his room, who therefore was in danger too of being put to death by his Father when the conspiracy was discovered.[9]

VII.
MU'TAMAD KHAN, 1627

The Mughal chronicler Mu'tamad Khan, author of Tuzuk-i Jahangiri (Memoirs of Jahangir), noting the death of Malik Ambar, wrote the following about him, his qualities, and reputation:

Intelligence now arrived of the death of Ambar the Abyssinian, in the 80th year of his age, on 31st *Urdibihisht*. This Ambar was a slave, but an able man. In warfare, in command, in sound judge-ment, and in administration, he had no rival or equal. He well

9. Edward Grey, ed., *The Travels of Pietro della Valle in India from the old English translation of 1664 by G. Havers* (London: Hakluyt Society, 1892), Vol. 2, 442–443.

understood that predatory (*kazzaki*) warfare, which in the language of the Dakhin is called *bari-giri*. He kept down the turbulent spirits of that country, and maintained his exalted position to the end of his life, and closed his career in honour. History records no other instance of an Abyssinian slave arriving at such eminence.[10]

VIII.
FUZUNI ASTARABADI, 1643

Mir Hashim Beg Fuzuni Astarabadi was a Persian poet and chronicler of the Adil Shahi court. He wrote his Fatuhat-i-Adil Shahi between 1640 and 1643. It is the most comprehensive account of Malik Ambar from the end of Ferishta's Tarik-i-Firishtah, which was completed in 1612, up until 1626. In the following section Astarabadi describes Ambar's petitioning of the Adil Shah, starting with Ambar's own words in approximately 1608:

"It is my design to fight the Mughal troops so long as life remains in this body. It may be that through Your Majesty's daily increasing fortune I shall expel the Mughals from the Deccan. But I have no place where I can deposit my children with composure of mind before engaging the enemy. It would not be far from your royal grace to grant me the fort of Qandahar, which your officers have captured again after the olden times." Adil Shah granted the prayer, and gave him that fort. When Ambar got possession of Qandahar, a splendor and strength was gained by him, and his power daily increased. When Emperor Jahangir recalled Khan-i-Khanan in displeasure, Ambar seized the opportunity, sent force, captured the fort of Antur, and put all its Mughal garrison to the sword. This feat made him the bolder in slaying Mughals . . .

---

10. Mu'tamad Khan, *Iqbal-nama-yi Jahangiri (Tuzuk-i Jahangiri*, Memoirs of Jahangir), in *History of India as Told by its Own Historians*, ed. and trans. Henry M. Elliot and John Dowson (Allahbad, 1964), Vol. 6: 428–429.

[With regard to the Mughals defeating Ambar in 1616] ... With the Habshi nobles and the Mughal army he marched to the bank of the river of Paitan. Every day Ambar's nobles used to come and fight like *bargis* and great battles took place. Spies reported to the Mughal general that Ambar himself was coming, with 40,000 horses ... The Mughals took post in a village encircled by the river of Paitan, with a deep ditch in front, behind which they planted their artillery. Next day Ambar appeared. His squadron of youths [*bachgan*, i.e. pages], ten thousand Habshis, of the age of 17 or 18, mounted on Persian horses, charged from the front of Ambar. They were caught by the deep ditch and could neither advance nor retreat, being huddled together as if they had been chained. In this position they were mown down by the Mughal artillery, like leaves of trees under a destroying wind ...

The right and left wings of Ambar fled away of themselves, due to their dissension with him. The Mughals then advanced to the attack, slaying many of his slaves. A great defeat and flight fell on Ambar's army. They were pursued for nearly one *farsakh* and their property plundered. So many elephants, horses and other kinds of property fell into the hands of the Mughal troops that they became rich ...

Shah Nawaz Khan burnt and totally desolated the country from Paitan to Khirki. The houses of Ambar were not allowed to be ravaged, but in the city of Khirki the devastation went beyond all limits. Ambar took refuge in Daulatabad fort. Peace was now made on condition of the Deccani Sultans paying 12 lakhs of *hun* to the prince, the nobles and Shah Nawaz Khan. The Mughal generals returned to their stations.

[With regard to the Battle of Bahtvadi] Ambar marched away towards his own dominions. Adil Shah sent a large force under Ikhlas Khan Habshi on the heels of Ambar . . . so that this army [advanced] from the front and Mulla Muhammad from behind. Ambar seeing himself surrounded by the tempest of calamity, left the road and with a few soldiers entered the strong fort of Bhatvadi, and gave repose to his soldiers. By [letting out] the water of the lake of Bhatvadi, he barred the path before the Mughal army [and] the abundance of mud and mire weakened the Mughal army, and though his own men were fewer, his heart remained confident in reliance upon God.

When Ambar fled into a nook, the Mughal army under Mulla Muhammad arrived near Bijapur . . . Ambar fled away and the armies of the three kings [Mughal, Adil Shah, and Qutub Shah] came up pursuing him.

The rainy season invested the ground with the mantle of water; the excess of mud and rain weakened both the armies. Scarcity of food reached an extreme point in the camps of the Mughals and Adil Shah. For two or three nights together the quadrupeds did not get any fodder; what could the men get? Things came to such a pass that strength for movement was not left in the bodies for men or beasts. At Mulla Muhammad's request, Adil Shah sent treasure and provisions, but the convoy after arriving near the frontier did not dare proceed further in fear of Ambar's troops. At this time, as in the Mughal army the soldiers did not get their pay and there was no food, many went over to Ambar-jiu, who welcomed, honored and fed them and took them into his service. At the report of this good treatment by Malik Ambar, many Mughal and Adil Shahi soldiers fled away at night to him and were cherished there, till it even happened that once a detachment of Ambar's troops, ten thousand horsemen strong, issued from their post, delivered a night attack on the Mughal camp, and came back to their place in the morning. This occurred repeatedly. Terror of Ambar's army seized the hearts of the enemies' troops, they spent their nights without sleep and their days without repose. Matters at last came to such a pass, that when Mulla Muhammad ordered any officer to go out and escort the treasure and provisions, nobody would agree to it, in terror . . . Ambar's strength daily increased and that of the Mughals decreased, till at last he gave up night-attacks and began to wage battles by day. On many days coming from one side he would plunder and slay a party and go back. As only two or three *kos* separated the rival camps, this side attacked that or that side this. At last Ambar planted his own tent and the Nizam Shahi royal standard (*nah-gazi*) in front of the Mughal army with great pomp and demonstration. The Mughal army was labouring under several difficulties from which Ambar's men were free: famine and hunger, disunion, two hearts, two languages, excess of rain—these ruined them.

A great disgrace fell upon the armies of the three [allied] kings . . . Malik Ambar swollen to greatness by this victory, from an ant into a snake, and enriched with wealth exceeding the treasures of Corah, and troops numerous beyond imagination, laid siege to Sholapur. When he brought the "Malik Maidan" gun there, the garrison capitulated. Two years after this Ambar died.[11]

11. Fuzuni Astarabadi, *Fatuhat-i-Adil Shahi*, 1640–1643, in British Museum, Add. 27, 251, in Jadunath Sarkar. *House of Shivaji, Studies and Documents on Maratha History: Royal Period* (Hyderabad: Orient Blackswan, 2012), 18–20.

STUDY QUESTIONS

1. How does King Phillip II view Malik Ambar in Document 1? Is Ambar portrayed as someone to be trusted to advance Iberian interests in the region? If so, how?

2. What is the underlying tone of Abu'l-Fazl ibn Mubarak in Document 2 with regard to Ambar? To whom is the document directed and in what ways is this evident?

3. How are Muhammad Qasim Ferishta's observations in Document 3 different from Abu'l-Fazl's in Document 2? Can they simply be attributed to differences in loyalties, or does the ten-year period— what happens during those intervening years—between the two documents make a difference?

4. What is Pieter van den Broecke's overall assessment of Ambar in Document 4? To what extent does it either corroborate or contradict other documents that speak to Ambar's accomplishments?

5. Is it possible to draw connections about Ambar's piety and his abilities as a military commander? If so, what can be drawn from what Mirza Asad Beg has to say in Document 5?

6. How does one explain the claims of "sorcery" made by Pietro della Valle in Document 6? Also, what can be gathered about Ambar's relationship with the Adil Shah?

7. What motives might Mu'tamad Khan have in writing about Ambar in such glowing terms? Can it be trusted given the largely negative ways in which Mughal chroniclers write about Ambar?

8. What are the strengths of Ambar's military maneuverings as portrayed by Fuzuni Astarabadi in Document 8?

FURTHER READING

Ali, Shanti Sadiq. *The African Dispersal in the Deccan: From Medieval to Modern Times*. Hyderabad: Orient Blacksburn, 2012.

Alpers, Edward A. "The Other Middle Passage: The African Slave Trade in the Indian Ocean," in *Many Middle Passages: Forced Migration and the Making of the Modern World*, Emma Christopher, Cassandra Pybus, and Marcus Rediker, eds. Berkeley: University of California Press, 2007.

Basu, Helene. "Slave, Soldier, Trader, Faqir: Fragments of African Histories in Western India (Gujarat)," in *The African Diaspora in the Indian Ocean*, Shihan de Silva Jayasuriya and Richard Pankhurst, eds. Trenton, NJ: The Red Sea Press, 2003.

Bulcha, Mukuria. *The Making of the Oromo Diaspora: A Historical Sociology of Forced Migration*. Minneapolis: Kirk House Publishers, 2002.

Chatterjee, Indrani, and Richard M. Eaton, eds. *Slavery and South Asian History*. Bloomington: Indiana University Press, 2006.

Chauhan, R. R. S. *Africans in India: From Slavery to Royalty*. New Delhi: Asian Publication Services, 1995.

Chowdhuri, Jogindra Nath. *Malik Ambar: A Biography Based on Original Sources*. Calcutta: M. C. Sarkar, 1933.

Eaton, Richard M. *A Social History of the Deccan, 1300–1761: Eight Indian Lives*. New York: Cambridge University Press, 2005.

Fukazawa, Hiroshi. *The Medieval Deccan: Peasants, Social Systems and States Sixteenth to Eighteenth Centuries*. New York: Oxford University Press, 1999.

Haidar, Navina Najat, and Maria Sardar, eds. *Sultans of Deccan India: 1500–1700: Opulence and Fantasy*. New York and New Haven, CT: Metropolitan Museum of Art and Yale University Press, 2015.

Jayasuriya, Shihan de Silva, and Richard Pankhurst, eds. *The African Diaspora in the Indian Ocean.* Trenton, NJ: Africa World Press, 2003.

Kapteijns, Lidwien. "Ethiopia and the Horn of Africa," in *The History of Islam in Africa,* Nehemia Levtzion and Randall Lee Pouwells, eds. Athens: Ohio University Press, 2000.

Kumar, Sunil. "Service, Status, and Military Slavery in the Delhi Sultanate: Thirteenth and Fourteenth Centuries," in *Slavery and South Asian History,* Indrani Chatterjee and Richard M. Eaton, eds. Bloomington: Indiana University Press, 2006.

Lewis, Bernard. *Race and Slavery in the Middle East: An Historical Enquiry.* New York: Oxford University Press, 1992.

Margariti, Eleni. *Aden and the Indian Ocean Trade: 150 Years in the Life of a Medieval Arabian Port.* Chapel Hill: University of North Carolina Press, 2007.

Metcalf, Barbara D., ed. *Islam in South Asia in Practice.* Princeton, NJ: Princeton University Press, 2010.

Metcalf, Barbara D., and Thomas R. Metcalf. *A Concise History of India.* New York: Cambridge University Press, 2002.

Michell, George, and Mark Zebrowski. *Architecture and Art of the Deccan Sultanates, Vol. 1.* New York: Cambridge University Press, 1999.

Pankhurst, Richard. *The Ethiopians: A History.* Oxford: Blackwell Publishing, 2001.

Pankhurst, Richard. *A Social History of Ethiopia: The Northern and Central Highlands from Early Medieval Times to the Rise of Emperor Tewodros II.* Trenton, NJ: Red Sea Press, 1992.

Pipes, Daniel. *Slave Soldiers and Islam: The Genesis of a Military System.* New Haven, CT: Yale University Press, 1981.

Prakash, Om. *European Commercial Enterprise in Pre-Colonial India.* New York: Cambridge University Press, 1998.

Prange, Sebastian R. "A Trade of No Dishonor: Piracy, Commerce, and Community in the Western Indian Ocean, Twelfth to Sixteenth

Century." *The American Historical Review*, Vol. 116, No. 5 (2011): 1269–1293.

Richards, John F. "Formulation and Imperial Authority under Akbar and Jahangir," in *Kinship and Authority in South Asia*, Muzaffar Alam and Sanjay Subrahmanyam, eds. New York: Oxford University Press, 1998.

Robbins, Kenneth X., and John McLeod, eds. *African Elites in India: Habshi Amarat*. Ahmedabad, India: Mapin Publishing, 2006.

Rotzer, Klaus. "The Architectural Legacy of Malik Ambar, Malik Sandal, and Yaqut Dabuli Habshi," in Kenneth X. Robbins and John McLeod, eds. *African Elites in India: Habshi Amarat*. Ahmedabad, India: Mapin Publishing, 2006.

Saksena, Banarasi Prasad. "A Few Unnoticed Facts about the Early Life of Malik Amber," in *Transactions of the Indian History Congress* 5, Hyderabad Session, 1941.

Sarkar, Jadunath. *House of Shivaji, Studies and Documents on Maratha History: Royal Period*. Hyderabad: Orient Blackswan, 2012.

Sheriff, Abdul. *Dhow Cultures of the Indian Ocean: Cosmopolitanism, Commerce and Islam*. New York: Columbia University Press, 2010.

Sherwani, H. K., and P. M. Joshi, eds. *History of Medieval Deccan, 1295–1724*. Hyderabad: Government of Andhra Pradesh, 1973.

Shulman, David. "On South Indian Bandits and Kings." *The Indian Economic and Social History Review*, Vol. 17, No. 3 (1980): 283–306.

Shyam, Radhey. *Life and Times of Malik Ambar*. Delhi: Munshiram Manoharlal, 1968.

Tamaskar, Bhaskar G. *The Life and Work of Malik Ambar*. Delhi: Idarah-i Adabiyat-i Delli, 1978.

Verma, Dinesh Chandra. *History of Bijapur*. Indian Institute of Islamic Studies. New Delhi: Kumar Bros., 1974.

Yimene, Ababu Minda. *An African Indian Community in Hyderabad: Siddi Identity, Its Maintenance, and Change*. Cuvilier Verlag: Gottingen, 2004.

NOTES

INTRODUCTION

1. Mu'tamad Khan, *Iqbal-nama-yi Jahangiri* (*Tuzuk-i-Jahangiri*, Memoirs of Jahangir), in *History of India as Told by its Own Historians*, Vol. 6, ed. and trans. Henry M. Elliot, and John Dowson, ed. (Allahabad, 1964), 428–429.
2. *Ibid.*; Muhammed Qasim Ferishta (*Tarikh-i-Ferishta*), *History of the Rise of the Mohammedan Power in India*, Vol. III, John Briggs, trans. (New York: Cambridge University Press, 2013), 315–317; W. Ph. Coolhaas, ed., *Pieter van den Broecke in Azië*, Vol. I (The Hague: Martinus Nijhoff, 1962), 146–151; Mirza Asad Beg, *Wakiat-i-Asad Beg*, in Indian History Congress, Proceedings (1941), 601–603; Pietro della Valle; Sivaji Nibandhavali, Vol. II, 13, quoted in Bhaskar G. Tamaskar, *The Life and Work of Malik Ambar* (Delhi: Idarah-i Adabiyat-i Delli, 1978), 317.

CHAPTER I

1. Herbert S. Lewis, "The Origins of the Galla and Somali," *Journal of African History*, VII, I (1966), 27–46; Richard Pankhurst, *The Ethiopians: A History* (Oxford: Blackwell Publishing, 2001); Abbah Bayhrey, *History of the Galla*, in C. F. Beckingham et al. *Some Records of Ethiopia, 1593–1646* (London: Hakluyt Society, 1954); Sihab ad-Din Ahmad bin 'Abd al-Qader bin Saleem bin Utman, Paul Lester Stenhouse, trans. *Futuh Al-Habasha: The Conquest of Abyssinia* (Hollywood, CA: Tsehai Publishers, 2003), xvii–xviii. N.B. The Oromo were historically referred to by outsiders as "Galla."
2. *Helee* are traditional songs of family and country sung by Oromo women.
3. Abu'l-Fazl ibn Mubarak, *The Akbarnama of Abu-l-Fazl*, Henry Beveridge, trans., Vol. 3 (Calcutta: Asiatic Society of Bengal, 1909), 1178; Fuzuni Astarabadi, *Fatuhat-i-Adil Shahi*, 1640–1643, in British Museum, Add. 27, 251, in Jadunath Sarkar, *House of Shivaji, Studies and Documents on Maratha History: Royal Period* (Hyderabad: Orient Blackswan, 2012), 18–20.
4. In Afaan Oromoo, an Eastern Cushitic language, "Shambhu" is used as both a personal and place name, as in the town of the same name west of Addis Ababa; Mukuria Bulcha, *The Making of the Oromo Diaspora: A Historical Sociology of Forced Migration* (Minneapolis: Kirk House Publishers, 2002), 117.
5. *Ibid.*, 47.

6. See Omar H. Ali, "Introduction" to "The African Diaspora in the Indian Ocean World," online exhibit, Schomburg Center for Research in Black Culture, The New York Public Library, 2011.

7. Marco Polo, among others, noted the use of Abyssinian military slaves, Ronald Latham, ed., *Marco Polo, The Customs of the Kingdom of India* (New York: Penguin, 2007), 15. See Daniel Pipes, *Slave Soldiers and Islam: The Genesis of a Military System* (New Haven, CT: Yale University Press, 1981), *passim*.

8. Ibn Battuta, Tim Mackintosh-Smith, ed., *The Travels of Ibn Battuta* (London: Picador, 2002), 216.

9. C. F. Beckinham and G. W. B. Huntingford, trans., *The Prester John of the Indies* (Cambridge: Hakluyt Society, 1961), Vol. 1, 320–321; see Pankhurst, 67.

10. Adding to the mix of faiths and people in Ethiopia are members of the centuries-old Ethiopian Jewish community, known as Beta Esra'el, scattered in the northwest.

11. Lidwien Kapteijns, "Ethiopia and the Horn of Africa," *The History of Islam in Africa*, Nehemia Levtzion and Randall Lee Pouwells, eds. (Athens: Ohio University Press, 2000), 230.

12. Part of the difference in treatment of captives among the Oromo is reflected in the relative dearth of words for "slavery" and "slave trade" in the Afaan Oromoo language in comparison to Amharic or Arabic—the languages used respectively by many Christian and Muslim Abyssinians. Bulcha, *The Making of the Oromo Diaspora*, 48; Asmarom Legesse, *Gada: Three Approaches to the Study of African Societies* (New York: Free Press, 1973), 8; Mohammed Hassen, *The Oromo of Ethiopia: A History 1570–1860* (New York: Cambridge University Press, 1990), 9–17.

13. Pankhurst,125.

14. Richard M. Eaton, *A Social History of the Deccan, 1300–1761: Eight Indian Lives* (London: Cambridge University Press, 2005), 107; Tomé Pires, *The Suma Oriental of Tomé Pires: An Account of the East from the Red Sea to Japan, Written in Malacca and India in 1512–1515*, trans. Armando Cortesao (London, 1944; repr. New Delhi, 1990), Vol. 1: 8.

15. Pankhurst, 115.

16. See Ali, "East Africa" essay in "The African Diaspora in the Indian Ocean World," 2011.

17. Radhey Shyam, *Life and Times of Malik Ambar*, 34–35, and Shanti Sadiq Ali, *The African Dispersal in the Deccan: From Medieval to Modern Times* (Hyderabad: Orient Blacksburn, 2012), 64, both state that Malik Ambar's parents sold him due to their poverty. By contrast, Satish Chandra and Richard Eaton suggest that he may have been sold or that he may have been captured in war; Chandra, *Medieval India: From Sultanate to the Mughals* (New Delhi: Har-Anand Publications, 1999), 196; Eaton, *A Social History of the Deccan, 1300–1761*, 105.

18. Ronald Segal, *Islam's Black Slaves: The Other Black Diaspora* (New York: Farrar, Straus, and Giroux, 2001), 154.
19. As the Ethiopian scholar Mekuria Bulcha also notes of Oromo female captives: "When her beauty faded and she was no longer considered attractive enough to serve as an object of physical pleasure, the female slave, Oromo or not, was consigned to a life of household drudgery." Bulcha, *The Making of the Oromo Diaspora*, 105.
20. *Ibid.*, 107. This feature of slavery in the predominantly Muslim Indian Ocean world was markedly different from the predominantly Christian-dominated Americas. By the time Ambar was captured, thousands of West and West-Central Africans—from Senegambia down to Angola—had already been forcibly migrated as chattel slaves to work on the sugar plantations and silver mines of colonial Latin America. Although many Atlantic world captives did rise through the ranks of their slave system, such as becoming overseers (notably, Olaudah Equiano), few wielded anywhere near the kind of power seen among male captives of African descent in the Indian Ocean world. See Olaudah Equiano, introduction by Vincent Carretta, *The Interesting Narrative and Other Writings* (New York: Penguin Books, 2003), 124. Slave rebel leaders and maroons (runaway slaves) exerted power and authority, but not within colonial society per se. See Omar H. Ali, "Benkos Biohó: African Maroon Leadership in New Grenada" in *Atlantic Biographies: Individuals and Peoples in the Atlantic World*, Mark Meuwese and Jeffrey Fortin, eds. (Boston, MA: Brill, 2014), 263–294, and collection of essays in Lauren Dubois and Julius S. Scott, eds. *Origins of the Black Atlantic* (New York: Routledge, 2010), 7–395.
21. As Edward Alpers notes regarding the "Middle Passage" in the African slave trade of the Indian Ocean, "passage from freedom into slavery . . . began with the moment in which they were swept up by the economic forces that drove the slave trade deep into the African interior"; Alpers, "The Other Middle Passage: The African Slave Trade in the Indian Ocean" in *Many Middle Passages: Forced Migration and the Making of the Modern World*, Emma Christopher, Cassandra Pybus, Marcus Rediker, eds. (Berkeley: University of California Press, 2007), 21.
22. Reconstructing Ambar's early life through contextualization and imagined scenes is part of a discursive strategy in writing about historical figures where documentary evidence is sparse. Among others, the historian Natalie Zemon Davis employs this strategy in her biography of the Granada-born diplomat Leo Africanus; *Trickster Travels: A Sixteenth Century Muslim between Worlds* (New York: Hill and Wang, 2006). See Jonathan P. Berkey's featured review of the book in *The American Historical Review*, Vol. 112, No. 2 (April 2007): 459–461.

CHAPTER 2

1. One ducat in the seventeenth century would have been roughly the equivalent of forty dollars today, meaning that Ambar was bought for approximately eight hundred dollars. The account of the sale of Ambar at Mocha comes from the Dutchman Peter Van Den Broecke, who spoke with him in India. W. Ph. Coolhaas, ed., *Pieter van dem Broecke in Azië* (The Hague: Martinus Nijhoff, 1962), 1:146–151, translated by J. W. Smit in *Africans Abroad: A Documentary History of the Black Diaspora in Asia, Latin America, and the Caribbean During the Age of Slavery*, Graham W. Irwin, ed. (New York: Columbia University Press, 1977), 153.

2. The name Hussein is largely associated with the Prophet Muhammad's grandson, Hussein Ibn Ali, who is among the most venerated figures among Shi'a for having been martyred at the Battle of Karbala in 680 C.E.

3. The grandeur of this particular Hajj was described by the Egyptian scholar Al-Umari, who noted that the massive influx of gold into Cairo (both as gifts and for trade) destabilized the price of the precious metal for no less than twelve years after the emperor passed through the city.

4. See introductory essay in Omar H. Ali, *Islam in the Indian Ocean World: A Brief History with Documents* (Boston: Bedford St. Martin's Press, 2016). *N.B.* Eastern Cushitic non-Muslims in Ethiopia tended to practice circumcision during this period, so it is very possible that Ambar was already circumcised—a practice among Muslims.

5. *Ibid.* As tradition goes, Bilal was tortured by his master (a polytheist and bitter opponent of Islam) for refusing to recant that there is only one god, *Allah*, and no other. Hearing of the determined Abyssinian, one of Muhammad's close companions, Abu Bakr, purchased and emancipated Bilal, who would go on to become Islam's first *mu'azzin* (the person who makes the call to prayer) and helped Muhammad lead the early Muslim community. Omar H. Ali, "The Muazzin's Song: Islam and the African Diaspora of the Indian Ocean World," *North Carolina Conversations*, Vol. 6, No. 1 (2012): 14–15.

6. Ibn Battuta, *Travels in Asia and Africa, 1325–1354* (London: Routledge, 1983), 78.

7. Baghdad boasted the largest concentration of Shi'a—the major-minority Muslim sect whose adherents believe in a different line of political and religious authority than the majority Sunni tradition. There were also a small number of Zoroastrians, many of whose relatives had migrated east with the Muslim takeover of Baghdad, and were subsequently called Parsis, "Persians," in India; and Jews, whose traders conducted business from Iberia to southern India.

8. Al-Jahiz, trans. by Vincent J. Cornell, *Kitab Fakhr As-Sudan 'Ala Al-Bidan; The Book of Pride of the Blacks over the Whites* (France Preston, 1981), 41.

9. *Ibid.*, 40.
10. Radhey Shyam, *Life and Times of Malik Ambar* (Delhi: Munshiram Manoharlal, 1968), 35.
11. Ababu Minda Yimene, *An African Indian Community in Hyderabad* (Gottingen: Cuvillier Verlag, 2004), 111.
12. Ibn al-Mujawir Tarick al-Mustabsir quoted in Roxani Eleni Margariti, *Aden and the Indian Ocean Trade: 150 Years in the Life of a Medieval Arabian Port* (Chapel Hill: University of North Carolina Press, 2007), 1.
13. Tamaskar, 156; Muslim merchants had long made their way to the Gujarati port of Cambay. However, by the sixteenth century the port had succumbed to the buildup of silt, with trade shifting to Surat.
14. Tamaskar, 155.
15. *Ibid.*, 159.

CHAPTER 3

1. See details on geography in Eaton, *A Social History of the Deccan*, 137.
2. Linguistically, within the borders of the Nizam Shahi, in addition to the majority Marathi speakers, followed by Persian and Dakhini speakers, there were Telugu speakers in the southeast and Kannad speakers in the south; Tamaskar, 335.
3. The term "Hindu" encompasses a great range of people and practices. As Aurobindo Ghosh (Sri Aurobindo) remarked, "Hinduism alone is by itself a vast and complex thing, not so much a religion as a great diversified and yet subtly unified mass of spiritual thought," in *Indian Philosophy in English: From Renaissance to Independence*, Nalini Bhushan and Jay L. Garfield, eds. (New York: Oxford University Press, 2012), 55.
4. There was great commonality and fluidity among people and their cultures across the Deccan and India as a whole; in this way, neither "Islam" nor "Hindu" was fixed, but they overlapped and grew with each other. See Barbara D. Metcalf and Thomas R. Metcalf, *A Concise History of India* (New York: Cambridge University Press, 2002); Sanjay Subrahmanyam, "Reflections on State-Making and History-Making in South India, 1500–1800," *Journal of the Economic and Social History of the Orient*, Vol. 41, No. 3 (1998): 383.
5. In 1486 the Sultan Jalaluddin Fath Shah of Bengal was overthrown by his chief eunuch, who was quickly overthrown by Shamsuddin Muzaffar Shah, a Habshi who was loyal to Jalaluddin. However, Shamsuddin was assassinated in 1493 for his brutal form of ruling. The result was the expulsion of Africans from Bengal. See R. R. S. Chauhan, *Africans in India: From Slavery to Royalty* (New Delhi: Asian Publication Services, 1995), 3.
6. Nizam al-Mulk, *The Book of Government or Book of Kings, The Siyāsat-nāma or Siyar al-Mulūk,* trans. Hubert Darke (New Haven, CT: Yale University Press, 1960), 121.

7. *The Travels of Ludovico di Varthema in Egypt, Syria, Arabia Deserta and Arabia Felix, In Persia, India, and Ethiopia*, A.D. 1503 to 1508, John Winter Jones, trans. (London: Hakluyt Society, 1863), 151.

8. Kenneth X. Robbins and John McLeod, eds. *African Elites in India: Habshi Amarat* (Ahmedabad, India: Mapin Publishing, 2006), 27.

9. See Richard Pankhurst, "Ethiopia Across the Red Sea and Indian Ocean: Ethiopian–Indian Relations in Ancient and Medieval Times," *Ethiopian Review*, May 14, 1999, and Richard Pankhurst, "The Ethiopian Diaspora to India," in *The African Diaspora in the Indian Ocean*, Shihan de Silva Jayasuriya and Richard Pankhurst, eds. (Trenton, NJ: Africa World Press, 2003), 189–217.

10. In addition to Afaan Oromoo, Ambar would have known Arabic from his years in Baghdad. In all he would have probably spoken at least four languages, including Dakhini, in addition to some Marathi, given the large number of Maratha in his army and the wider realm.

11. Metcalf, 8.

12. See Eaton, 59–60.

13. The Imad Shahi of Berar was overtaken by the Nizam Shahi of Ahmednagar in 1572, while Barid Shahi of Bidar was overtaken by the Adil Shahi of Bijapur in 1619.

14. "Mughal" being a derivative of 'Mongol.'

15. The Mughals were also concerned over the growing Portuguese presence on the western coast of India, arguing that only they were capable of keeping the Europeans at bay. Ambar would work with the Portuguese to push the Mughals back.

16. The same concept of military slavery could also be seen in the extensive employment of eunuchs in the Chinese imperial court. See Thomas Christensen, *1616: The World in Motion* (Berkeley, CA: Counterpoint), 279.

17. Eaton, *A Social History of the Deccan*, 106.

18. See Edwin Binney, "Indian Paintings from the Deccan," *Journal of the Royal Society of the Arts*, Vol. 127, No. 5280 (November 1979): 784–804; Robbins and McLeod, eds., *African Elites in India: Habshi Amarat* (Ahmedabad, India: Mapin Publishing, 2006), *passim*.

19. Eaton, *A Social History of the Deccan*, 120.

20. See Eaton, *A Social History of the Deccan*, 125–126; Dror Ze'evi, "My Son, my Lord: Slavery, Family and State in the Islamic Middle East," in Toru and Philips, eds. *Slaves Elites*, 4, 76.

21. Eaton, *A Social History of the Deccan*, 114. The notion survives in English today as someone being "true to the salt"—an Indian influence on Britain through the latter's former colonial connection.

22. For further explanation on the concept of "fidelity to salt" in South Asia see Sunil Kumar, "Service, Status, and Military Slavery in the Delhi Sultanate: Thirteenth and Fourteenth Centuries," in *Slavery and South Asian History*, Indrani Chatterjee and Richard M. Eaton, eds. (Bloomington: Indiana University Press, 2006), 82–114, and John F. Richards, "Formulation and Imperial Authority under Akbar

and Jahangir," in *Kinship and Authority in South Asia*, Muzaffar Alam and Sanjay Subrahmanyam, eds. (New York: Oxford University Press, 1998), 126–167.

CHAPTER 4

1. Chowdhuri, 17.
2. Eaton further observes, "In Malik Ambar's own case, it was only the Dutchman Van den Broecke, an outsider whose own culture drew a severe distinction between the categories of slave and free, who mentioned the Ethiopian's manumission by Chengiz Khan's widow. Persian chronicles made no notice of Malik Ambar's manumission, nor of that of other Habshi slaves," Eaton, 125–126.
3. Shyam, *Life and Times of Malik Ambar*, 36.
4. Robbins and McLeod, eds., *African Elites in India*, 90.
5. Sarkar, *House of Shivaji*; Ali, *The African Dispersal in the Deccan*, 104.
6. Robbins and McLeod, eds., *African Elites in India*, 33.
7. Robbins and McLeod, eds., *African Elites in India*, 33; Verma, *History of Bijapur*, 248–249.
8. Eaton, 115; Coolhaas, *Pieter Van den Broecke*, I:148.
9. Sadiq Ali, *The African Dispersal in the Deccan*, 59.
10. Bhaskar G. Tamaskar, *The Life and Work of Malik Ambar* (Delhi: Idrah-I Adabiyat-I, 1978), 34–35.
11. "The Siege of Ahmadnagar," translation by Major J. S. King of Sayyid Ali bin Azizullah Tabataba's *Burhan-i-Masir*, *The Indian Antiquary*, Vol. 27 (September 1898), 234; Sadiq Ali, *The African Dispersal in the Deccan*, 61.
12. *Ibid.*
13. Tamaskar, *The Life and Work of Malik Ambar*, 35.
14. Shyam, *Life and Times of Malik Ambar*, 37; Eaton, 115.
15. Ferishta, *Tarikh-i-Ferishta*, 302; see also Tamaskar, *The Life and Work of Malik Ambar*, 40.
16. Tamaskar, *The Life and Work of Malik Ambar*, 41; Eaton, *A Social History of the Deccan*, 113.
17. Eaton, *A Social History of the Deccan*, 113–114.

CHAPTER 5

1. Abu'l-Fazl, *Akbarnama*, Vol. 3, 1159.
2. Banditry on land was an extension of piracy at sea in the western Indian Ocean world. Both were respectively institutionalized and socially recognized as part of South Asia's caste system and re-counted in folklore. As David Shulman notes, "In South Asia, a bandit is . . . not 'made' but rather born as such." See Shulman, "On South Indian Bandits and Kings," *The Indian Economic and Social History Review*, Vol. 17, No. 3 (1980), 283–306; Sebastian R. Prange, "A Trade of No Dishonor: Piracy, Commerce, and Community in the Western Indian Ocean, Twelfth to Sixteenth Century," *The American*

Historical Review, Vol. 116, No. 5 (2011): 1269–1293. For a discussion of forms of banditry in a wider world-historical context, see Sylviane Diouf, *Slavery's Exiles: The Story of the American Maroons* (New York: New York University Press, 2014), 230–236.

3. Eaton, *A Social History of the Deccan*, 115; Sarkar, *House of Shivaji*, 6–7.
4. Shyam, *Life and Times of Malik Ambar*, 38–39; Eaton, *A Social History of the Deccan*, 115–116.
5. Sarkar, *House of Shivaji*, 7–8; Eaton, *A Social History of the Deccan*, 115–118.
6. Radhey Shyam, *The Kingdom of Ahmednagar* (Delhi: Motilal Banarsidass, 1966), 1.
7. Ferishta, *Tarikh-i-Ferishta*, 315–316; in Qandahar, the Mughals describe how "if the men of right and left wing had extended the arms of courage, the enemy would not have escaped, and 'Ambar . . . would certainly have been made prisoner," Abu'l-Fazl, *Akbarnama*, Vol. 3, 1223.
8. Tamaskar, *The Life and Work of Malik Ambar*, 47, 171.
9. Tamaskar, *The Life and Work of Malik Ambar*, 77–78.
10. Abu'l-Fazl, *Akbarnama*, Vol. 3, 1258.
11. Indu Sundaresan, *The Feast of Roses: A Novel* (New York: Washington Square Press, 2004), 131–132.
12. Tamaskar, *The Life and Work of Malik Ambar*, 62–63; Ferishta, *Tarikh-i-Ferishta*, 315–317.
13. Nawab Samsam al-Daulah Shahnawaz Khan and Abdul Hai Khan, *The Ma'asir-ul-Umara, Biographies of the Muhammadan and Hindu Officers of the Timurid Sovereigns of India from 1500 to about 1780 A.D.*, trans. Henry Beveridge and Baini Prashad (Calcutta: Asiatic Society of Bengal, 1911), Vol. 1, 277.
14. Muhammed Qasim Ferishta (*Tarikh-i-Ferishta*), *History of the Rise of the Mohammedan*, 315–317, 320.
15. Eaton, *A Social History of the Deccan*, 118.
16. Tamaskar, *The Life and Work of Malik Ambar*, 182, 196, 198 endnote 7; Finch (1610) in Robert Kerr, *A General History and Collection of Voyages and Travels*, VIII (London: T. Cadell), 280.
17. Shyam, *Life and Times*, 72.
18. *Ibid.*, 73–75.
19. See Eaton, 119.
20. Christensen, *1616: World in Motion*, 280.
21. With assistance from Daniel Prinz, the translation comes from W. Ph. Coolhaas, ed., *Pieter van den Broecke in Azië* (The Hague: Martinus Nijhoff, 1962), 1:146–151, in Graham W. Irwin, *Africans Abroad: A Documentary History of the Black Diaspora in Asia, Latin America, and the Caribbean During the Age of Slavery* (New York: Columbia University Press, 1977), 152–155.
22. Richard Eaton, "Women's Grinding and Spinning Songs of Devotion in the Late Medieval Deccan," in Barbara D. Metcalf, ed., *Islam in*

South Asia in Practice (Princeton, NJ: Princeton University Press, 2010), 90–91. The *"chakki* (grindstone) song" combines the different parts of a grindstone with basic Islamic precepts.

23. Ferishta, *Tarikh-i-Ferishta*, 315–317.

CHAPTER 6

1. Henry M. Elliot, *The History of India*, Vol. 6 (London: Trübner and Co., 1877), 333–334; Mu'tamad Khan, *Tuzuk-i-Jahangiri*, 292.
2. Mirza Asad Beg, *Wakiat-i-Asad Beg*, in Indian History Congress, Proceedings, 1941, 601–603.
3. Shyam, *Life and Times*, 149–150.
4. Pietro della Valle quoted in Bhaskar G. Tamaskar, *The Life and Work of Malik Ambar* (Delhi: Idarah-i Adabiyat-i Delli, 1978), 317. The accusation against Africans in Asia of using sorcery has a number of precedents, as in the story of "Aladdin and the Wonderful Lamp," in which he is tricked by a "wicked" African magician; Muhsin al-Musawi, *The Arabian Nights*, introduction and notes based on the French translation by Antoine Galland (New York: Barnes and Noble Classics, 2007), 522–622. There are also positive stories in Arabic lore of Africans with special powers, such as rainmakers. See Muhammad ibn Sasra, *A Chronicle of Damascus 1389–1397*, W. M. Brinner, ed. and trans. (Berkeley and Los Angeles: University of California Press, 1963) Vol. 1, 278; Graham W. Irwin, *Africans Abroad: A Documentary History of the Black Diaspora* (New York: Columbia University Press, 1977), 61–62.
5. Mu'tamad Khan, *Tuzuk-i-Jahangiri*, Vol. 1, 275; Elliot and Dowson, *History of India as Told by her own Historians*, VI, 340; Tamaskar, *The Life and Work of Malik Ambar*, 93.
6. Tamaskar, *The Life and Work of Malik Ambar*, 122. In addition to assassination attempts, there were directives to capture Ambar, as in 1607 when Jahangir sent a force to capture him; Yimene, 113; Pankhurst, 1972, 111.
7. Tamaskar, *The Life and Work of Malik Ambar*, 313–314.
8. Abu'l-Fazl, *Ain-i Akbari*, trans. Henry Blochmann, Vol. 1 (Calcutta: Royal Asiatic Society, 1873), 503.
9. Abu'l-Fazl, *Akbarnama*, Vol. 3, 1178.
10. Elliot, *The History of India*, Vol. 6, 333–334; Mu'tamad Khan, *Tuzuk-i-Jahangiri*, 292.
11. Joannes de Laet, *The Empire of The Empire of the Great Mogol, A Translation of De Laet's "Description of India and Fragment of Indian History,"* John S. Hoyland, trans. (Bombay: D. B. Taraporevala Sons & Co., 1928), 185–188; see also *A Contemporary Dutch Chronicle of Mughal India*, trans. Brij Narain and Sri Ram Sharma (Calcutta: Susil Gupta India Limited, 1957), 45–46.
12. Tamaskar, *The Life and Work of Malik Ambar*, 286; François Pyrard de Laval, *Travels to the East Indies, the Moluccas, and Brazil* (London:

Hakluyt Society, 1890), Vol. 2, 257–258; *The Voyage of François Pyrard de Laval, to the East Indies, the Maldives, the Moluccas and Brazil.*

13. Abu'l-Fazl, *Akbarnama*, Vol. 3, 1209.

14. Ferishta, *Tarikh-i-Ferishta*, 316.

15. Shyam, *Life and Times*, 149–150.

16. Abu'l-Fazl, *Akbarnama*, Vol. 3, 1212.

17. In addition to *bargis*, there were two other kinds of mounted warriors in the Deccan: *silehdars*, which were "mail-clad" knights, and generally less reliable than *bargis*, and the horsemen maintained by local feudal chiefs, which Ambar seldom enlisted; Shyam, *Life and Times*, 149–150.

18. Klaus Rotzer, "The Architectural Legacy of Malik Ambar, Malik Sandal, and Yaqut Dabuli Habshi," in Robbins and McLeod, eds., *African Elites in India*, 90.

19. Shyam, *Life and Times*, 149–150.

20. Ibn Battuta, Tim Mackintosh-Smith, ed., *The Travels of Ibn Battuta* (London: Picador, 2002), 216.

21. Ali, "East Africa" essay in "The African Diaspora in the Indian Ocean World," 2011.

22. Tamaskar, *The Life and Work of Malik Ambar*, 156; Sidi Ambar would govern until 1641, at which time Sidi Yusuf took over; see "The Sidi Kingdom of Janjira," Robbins and McLeod, *African Elites in India*, 179, 213.

23. Eaton, *A Social History of the Deccan*, 129.

24. Extracts from *Asad-i Waqiat* in Banarasi Prasad Saksena in *Proceedings, Indian History Congress*, 5 (Hyderabad, 1941), 601–603; Tamaskar, *The Life and Work of Malik Ambar*, 66–67, 75.

25. Tamaskar, *The Life and Work of Malik Ambar*, 67.

26. Shyam, *Life and Times*, 102–103; Mu'tamad Khan, *Tuzuk-i-Jahangiri*, Vol. 2, 208.

CHAPTER 7

1. Here I am closely paraphrasing the great twentieth-century African-American historian and political activist W. E. B. Du Bois, who described Southern black farmers and sharecroppers—the peasant workers of the American South—as laborers who (as it were, some three centuries after Ambar's time and on the other side of the world) "bow and bend beneath the burden of it all"; *The Souls of Black Folk* (Chicago: A. C. McClure, 1903), 154.

2. James C. Scott, *Domination and the Arts of Resistance: Hidden Transcripts* (New Haven, CT: Yale University Press, 1990), 199.

3. Richard Eaton, "Women's Grinding and Spinning Songs of Devotion in the Late Medieval Deccan," in Barbara D. Metcalf, ed., *Islam in South Asia in Practice* (Princeton, NJ: Princeton University Press, 2010), 90–91.

NOTES 143

4. Among the region's many different kinds of peasants there were two types of cultivators: the *mirasdar*, who had relatively well-established proprietary land rights, and the tenant farmers, *upari* ("outsiders"), who rented land from the state, the village body, or feudal lords (nobles who were given a *jagir*, land grant, for their administrative or military services by a monarch). Peasant cultivators, who rented the land they worked and on which they lived, kept about half of the crops they yielded (or reported to have yielded) while handing over the remainder—to be sure reluctantly, as the share was onerous and did not, by and large, allow them to save for the future. Cultivators paid approximately one third of their yields to cover a range of taxes—a heavy burden to families and communities, who like their counterparts in other parts of India and the world become increasingly in debt, and therefore tied to their circumstances and landowners (*zamindar*); Tamaskar, *The Life and Work of Malik Ambar*, 341.

5. Hiroshi Fukazawa, *The Medieval Deccan: Peasants, Social Systems, and States, Sixteenth to Eighteenth Centuries* (Delhi: Oxford University Press, 1998), xii–xiii, 6.

6. Astarabadi, *Fatuhat-i-Adil Shahi*, in Sarkar, *House of Shivaji*, 15–17.

7. Mu'tamad Khan, *Tuzuk-i-Jahangiri*, Vol. 2, 36–37; Tamaskar, *The Life and Work of Malik Ambar*, 108.

8. Tamaskar, *The Life and Work of Malik Ambar*, 108.

9. *Ibid.*, 108–110.

10. Shyam, *The Kingdom of Ahmednagar*, 265.

11. Fuzuni Astarabadi, *Futuhat-i-Adil Shahi*, quoted in Tamaskar, *The Life and Work of Malik Ambar*, 131.

12. See Edward Grey, ed., *The Travels of Pietro della Valle in India from the old English translation of 1664 by G. Havers* (London: Hakluyt Society, 1892), Vol. 2, 442–443; Tamaskar, *The Life and Work of Malik Ambar*, 132; Sadiq Ali, *The African Dispersal in the Deccan*, 79–80.

13. Fuzuni Astarabadi, *Fatuhat-i-Adil Shahi*, 1640–1643, in British Museum, Add. 27, 251, in Sarkar, *House of Shivaji*, 18–20.

14. Astarabadi, *Fatuhat-i-Adil Shahi*, in Sarkar, *House of Shivaji*, 15–17.

15. Syed Ali bin Azizullah Tabataba, *Burhan-i-Masir*, in *Indian Antiquary*, 1923, 335–336.

16. Sadiq Ali, *The African Dispersal in the Deccan*, 61.

17. Tamaskar, *The Life and Work of Malik Ambar*, 284; Ferishta, *Tarikh-i-Ferishta*, 199, 201.

18. Ferishta, *History of the Rise of the Mahomedan Power*, 317.

19. Dilip Chitre, trans., *Says Tuka: Selected Poetry of Tukaram* (New Delhi, 1991), 21, 115; Eaton, 129, 134. According to tradition, Sant Tukaram threw his manuscripts into the Indrayani River, believing that they were keeping him from properly pursuing the spiritual path on which he had set out. The pages miraculously reappeared out of the river completely dry some two weeks later. See Eaton, *A Social History of the Deccan*, 137.

CHAPTER 8

1. Pieter Gillis van Ravesteyn, *The Rise of Western Quarters of the East India Company (Suratte, Arabia, and Persia)*, Heert Terpstra, ed. (The Hague: 1918); *The Quarterly of the Bharat Itihas Sanshodhak Mandal*, Puna, Vol. XI, No. 1; Bhaskar G. Tamaskar, *The Life and Work of Malik Ambar*, 301.

2. W. Ph. Coolhaas, ed., *Pieter van den Broecke in Azië* (The Hague: Martinus Nijhoff, 1962), 1:146–151.

3. Bhaskar G. Tamaskar, "An Estimate of Malik Ambar," *The Quarterly Review of Historical Studies*, Vols. 7–9, The Institute of Historical Studies, 1968, 249; Ferishta, *Tarikh-i-Ferishta*, 401–402.

4. In addition to the Qur'an, Ambar likely followed the Hadith, the written compilation of sayings and examples of the Prophet Muhammed and the early Muslim community.

5. The *Raj-Sabha*, reserved for only a few cases, was mostly adjudicated by government officials, with the sultan himself being the highest court of appeal; Tamaskar, *The Life and Work of Malik Ambar*, 226–228, 231, 235, 239; the *Gotsabha* is similar to the *Panchayats* in modern India.

6. Shyam, *The Kingdom of Ahmednagar*, 284–285; Tamaskar, *The Life and Work of Malik Ambar*, 294–295.

7. Tamaskar, *The Life and Work of Malik Ambar*, 295–296.

8. Ferishta, *Tarikh-i-Ferishta*, 401–402.

9. Tamaskar, *The Life and Work of Malik Ambar*, 89–90.

10. Astarabadi, *Fatuhat-i-Adil Shahi*, in Sarkar, *House of Shivaji*, 18–20.

11. Jagindra Nath Chowdhuri, *Malik Ambar: A Biography Based on Original Sources*, 27; *Tarikh-i-Shvaji* folio 6b (R.A.S. Ms.) translated by Jadunath Sarkar in *Modern Review* Vol. 1 (January–June, 1907).

12. Quoted in Eaton, 122; Mu'tamad Khan, *Iqbal-nama-yi Jahangiri (Tuzuk-i Jahangiri)*, in *History of India as Told by its Own Historians*, ed. and trans. Henry M. Elliot and John Dowson (Allahabad, 1964), Vol. 6: 428–429.

13. Ferishta, 320; Tamaskar, *The Life and Work of Malik Ambar*, 315.

14. Tamaskar notes that "[Ambar's] entrails were entombed at Ambarpur and other remains of his corpse were brought and cremated in another tomb at Roza," signifying the love and respect that both Muslims and Hindus had for him, as both burial and cremation were used; Tamaskar, *The Life and Work of Malik Ambar*, 142.

15. Rotzer, "The Architectural Legacy of Malik Ambar," in Robbins and McLeod, eds., *African Elites in India*, 90.

16. *Ibid.* See also, Navina Najat Haidar and Maria Sardar, eds., *Sultans of Deccan India: 1500–1700: Opulence and Fantasy* (New York and New Haven, CT: Metropolitan Museum of Art and Yale University Press, 2015), *passim*.

17. Shahnawaz Khan, *The Ma'asir-ul-Umara*, 536. *Kos* were units of distance used in India through the early modern period, each *ko* being the equivalent of approximately two miles.

18. Carl W. Ernst and Bruce B. Lawrence, *Sufi Martyrs of Love: The Chishti Order in South Asia and Beyond* (New York: Palgrave Macmillan, 2002), 21, 93.
19. Quoted in Tamaskar, *The Life and Work of Malik Ambar*, 319, endnote 27.
20. Eaton, *A Social History of the Deccan*, 106.
21. Elliot, *The History of India*, Vol. 6, 432.
22. Rotzer, 90.
23. Robbins and McLeod, 43, endnote 11; Promod B. Gadre, *Cultural Archeology of Ahmednagar during the Nizam Shahi Period (1494–1632)* (Delhi, 1986), 124–125.
24. See Riksum Kazi, "From African Slave to Deccani Military and Political Leader: Examining Malik Ambar's Life and Legacy," *The College of New Jersey Journal of Student Scholarship*, Vol. 14 (April 2012), 5.
25. Sarkar, *House of Shivaji*, 10.
26. *Ibid.*, 18.

EPILOGUE

1. Despite the renaming of Khirki first and very briefly to Fatehnagar (after Ambar's son Fateh Khan) in 1627 and then to Aurangabad in 1653, there is a vibrant oral tradition of Ambar's role in having founded the city. Oral interviews conducted in Aurangabad and Daulatabad, March 10–12, 2012, by Omar H. Ali.
2. Ambar's descendants are scattered across the Deccan. Ambar's eldest son Fateh Khan received a pension after surrendering to the Mughals. It is unclear what happened to his second son, Chengiz Khan. His daughter Shahir went to Nanded in Marathwada, where her tomb may be found. His other daughter, Azija, married Siddi Abdulah, who was given a *jagir* in the village of Velup, also in Nanded. Other descendants may be found in the regions surrounding Ahmednagar; see Sadiq Ali, *The African Dispersal in the Deccan*, 104. Today, Siddis in India live in Gujarat, the area of Janjira, as well as in Karnataka and Hyderabad (they also live in southern Pakistan and Sri Lanka); see Bindu Malieckal, "India's Luso-Africans: The Politics of Race, Colonialism, and Gender in Early Modern Portugal and Post-Colonial Goa" in *Religion and Politics in a Global Society: Comparative Perspectives from the Portuguese-Speaking World*, Paul Christopher Manuel, Alynna Lyon, and Clyde Wilcox, eds. (Lanham, MD: Lexington Books, 2013), 48. The anthropologist Helene Basu has explored the Siddis of Gujarat; see Basu, "Slave, Soldier, Trader, Faqir: Fragments of African Histories in Western India (Gujarat)," in *The African Diaspora in the Indian Ocean*, Shihan de Silva Jayasuriya and Richard Pankhurst, eds. (Trenton, NJ: The Red Sea Press, 2003), 223–249.

CREDITS

INDEX